Christie -

Keep Crushing it !

I

Success Hackers

CONVERSATIONS WITH ELITE
PERFORMERS
WHO HAVE CRACKED THE
ENTREPRENEURIAL CODE

Scott Hansen
Claudia Harvey
C.J. Seestadt
Chris Webb
Keith Kriegler
Rachel Nielsen
John Bates
Pritesh Gandhi
James Adamitis
Kathryn Janicek

Copyright © 2016 T. Allen Hanes Publishing Group

All rights reserved. No portion of this book may be reproduced--mechanically, electronically, or by any other means without the expressed written permission of the authors except as provided by the United States of America copyright law.

Published by T. Allen Hanes Publishing Group, Houston, TX

The Publisher has strived to be as accurate and complete as possible in the creation of this book.

This book is not intended for use as a source of legal, business, accounting or financial advice. All readers are advised to seek services of competent professionals in legal, business, accounting, and financial fields.

In practical advice books, like anything else in life, there are no guarantees of income made. Readers are cautioned to rely on their own judgment about their individual circumstances and to act accordingly.

While all attempts have been made to verify information provided in this publication, the Publisher assumes no responsibility for errors, omissions, or contrary interpretation of the subject matter herein. Any perceived slights of specific persons, peoples, or organizations are unintentional.

ISBN# **978-1530072415**

Manufactured & Printed in the United States of America.

Editor: Paul Jeff

Cover Design: Jim Villaflores

Publisher: T. Allen Hanes Publishing Group

"Success Hack" is a belief, a philosophy around achievement. It's taking an antiquated philosophy and turning it on its head. Success Hackers are the brave entrepreneurs who are always questioning the way "things ought to be", and then blazing their own trail. —Scott Hansen

If you were to ask one hundred people how many of them want to be more successful, increase their wealth, spend more time with their family, become more influential, or find their purpose, every person's hand would go up.

Yet, why is it that only a small fraction of the population would say that they are successful, and lead a life on purpose?
And those individuals who have achieved success, what is it that they do differently from everyone else?

I've been obsessed with these questions for the past 15 years

Chasing after your dreams, being your own boss, pursuing your purpose, standing out from the crowd, and impacting the world isn't for the faint of heart.

It takes an insane level of commitment and persistence; along with a belief in yourself when nobody else will.

When all the odds seem to be stacked against you, it's the ability to drown out all the noise and stay focused on your true desire.

When I made the leap from working in the corporate world,

to pursuing my passion of becoming a high-performance coach, speaker, and entrepreneur, there were doubts and fears that at times, seemed almost insurmountable. There were many times when I wanted to quit, throw in the towel, and go back to my old life. As I went through these moments, I would always go back to the same question, "when I'm 90 years old, sitting in my rocking chair, do I want to look back on my life and wonder, what could have been if I would've only pursued my dreams?"

Do you want to be remembered as someone who went after their dreams, made some noise, and was "all-in"; or someone who simply played it safe because you were afraid you might fail?

This book was born from my wildly successful podcast that bears the same name. The Success Hackers podcast is one of the fastest growing entrepreneurial podcasts in iTunes, and is downloaded and listened to by individuals in 65 countries. The guests that come on my show share their strategies, golden nuggets, and success hacks with our "Hacker Nation" community of entrepreneurs.

When coming up with the concept for this book, I thought it was important to have a variety of successful entrepreneurs from all different industries, with various backgrounds, share their philosophies and "success hacks", so that you can take what you read here and apply some of these strategies in your business.

Throughout this book there is a common underlying message: Failure is necessary.

Failure is good.

Failure will be the reason that stops you from your ultimate success, or you will use it as fuel to your success fire.

As you will experience, the entrepreneurs are featured in this book, as well as all high performers in the world, are great solution providers and problem solvers. The greater solution they pro-vide for various problems, the more money they make, the more influence they have, and ultimately the greater the impact they make across the world.

You might be asking, what is a Success Hacker?

In the Entrepreneurial world, there's a term that most entrepreneurs are striving to attain. That word is being a successful "entrepreneurial Hacker"; simply put, being a Success Hacker is learning and applying the short-cuts to your business

In the 19th century, it took John D Rockefeller, the oil tycoon 46 years to make $1bn.

In the late 2000s, it took Andrew Mason two years to do the same at Groupon.

The same can be said of Uber. Uber came and disrupted the taxi cab industry that has been around forever. Within a matter of a few years, at the writing of this book, Uber's valuation is $50bn.

A "success hack" is a belief, a philosophy around achievement. It's taking an antiquated philosophy and turning it on its head. Success Hackers are the brave entrepreneurs who are constantly questioning the way "things ought to be", and then blazing their own trail.

You are about to "peek behind the curtain" of some incredibly successful Entrepreneurs; to learn from their successes and failures. Some of their stories you may resonate with, some you may not. But in the end, you will learn some "Success hacks or smart-cuts" that can help you shorten the learning curve in your Entrepreneurial journey.

Scott Hansen

High-Performance Coach

Success Leaves Clues

Like many entrepreneurs, Scott has tried a bunch of different businesses; from networking marketing, to online marketing, and many others.

He was working at a full-time job while he was building a coaching business. After about six months, he decided to quit his job and dove head first into being a full-fledged entrepreneur. When he finally found his passion, there wasn't going to be any more starts and stops. Scott began to create and build a personal

1

development company that encompasses coaching, speaking, and podcasting; at that point he finally found his purpose.

As a high-performance coach, Scott works with entrepreneurs to help them become the very best versions of themselves while helping them grow their business.

He does that through many strategies and techniques.

Throughout the year, Scott offers "scholarships" to his potential clients; giving them the opportunity to experience a *Business Breakthrough* strategy session. During this deep coaching session, Scott works with a business owner, helping them understand what factors might be holding them back from achieving their ultimate success. Once he figures that out, he designs a game plan and strategy to help them build a bigger bottom line in their business

He also helps business owners who are spending too much time at work, to clarify & prioritize their focus so that they can make more money and work as little as they want.

Scott's "magic" is his ability to ask very deep, thought-provoking questions so he can get to the root of what's taking place inside the minds and hearts of his clients. Once he gets to this level, he creates strategies on how his clients can become more dominant in their industry, build a successful business, and live a life of significance.

He has always been drawn to HOW people got the results they got. Over time, he became fascinated with how some individuals were worth millions of dollars while others were barely getting by. He studied this subject voraciously for years.

After getting certified as a coach, he jumped in and never looked back. To be able to help/coach individuals to live a life of abundance, prosperity, and purpose is truly one of the most incredible feelings in the world.

Conversation with Scott Hansen

All right, thanks again for spending time with us Scott. I was just going to get right into it. Tell us about your business and what types of clients that you help?

Scott Hansen: I get the opportunity to help individuals, specifically Entrepreneurs, take the lid off their thinking; coaching them to play bigger in both life and business. As we embark upon adulthood, we stop taking risks, stop taking chances, and we stay in our comfort zone. Unfortunately, when we stay in our comfort zone, we deprive ourselves of achieving greatness in all areas of life.

As a high performance coach, it's my responsibility to help my clients "10x" the way they view themselves and their business. I coach them to find their passion, pursue their purpose, and ultimately to grow their business by impacting more people with their message. Coaching my clients involve working with them in a few areas: sharpening their skills, developing a high performer's mindset; all while getting crystal clear on what success means to them. Believe it or not, most people don't know what their definition of success is. During our very first coaching session, the first thing we do is find out what they want to achieve and why they want to achieve it. From there we design a game plan and a road map on how they can reach their overall success. We have one shot at this thing called life, and I'm a big believer that life is both very precious, and yet very fragile.

Doing something you are passionate about, and then being able to create wealth around this passion, is the ultimate goal that a lot of my clients want to accomplish.

That's perfect, when you say entrepreneur, that's a broad definition. I'm not sure if the audience knows what you mean by the entrepreneur. Could you go in deeper on exactly who you would help? Who would come to you and ask for help?

Scott Hansen: Regardless of whether or not they operate an online business or a more traditional "brick and mortar" business, the individuals I coach are CEOs and owners who've been in business for more than a few years, and they feel like they've hit a plateau. The natural areas of concern are: "how do I grow my business, how do I double or even triple my revenue, how do I empower and impact more people, or how can I become more productive throughout my day?" Having a coach or mentor becomes their ultimate accountability partner. A lot of times my clients already have the answer on what they need to do, it just takes someone like myself to draw that out. That's the impact that coaching can have on someone.

Before becoming an Entrepreneur, my background was in sales and leadership for over 15 years. Although I had what some might consider a fairly successful career, I always knew I was meant to do something different. People would always say to me "Scott, you would be effective in making this your career/business; coaching and empowering people to play bigger in their life and business." While I was working in the corporate world, I started to build my coaching business part-time, on the side. A few months later, after becoming a certified coach, trainer and speaker from the John Maxwell organization, I decided to quit my job and pursue the coaching business full time. Looking back, I probably should've waited another 6-12 months before I quit my job; until I had a steady base of clients, and the cash flow was consistent. But, I was so passionate about building this business; I knew that if I jumped out of the plane, it would force me to build the wings on the way down. When you dive into the deep end of the pool, you have two choices: you can learn how to swim, or drown.

Along the way, I've talked to a lot of entrepreneurs. There's always been a book that stands out that you might have read along the way that inspired you. Do you recall one of those books?

Scott Hansen: *"Think and Grow Rich"* was the book that opened my eyes to how rich and influential people thought differently than everyone else about creating wealth, prosperity, and abundance. Another excellent book was *"The Magic of Thinking Big"*. I also had the audio versions of these books. Anytime I would be driving in my car, I was listening to one of these CDs. I also read books and listened to CDs by Anthony Robbins. I started to realize that I was thinking way too small for my life. It doesn't take any more effort to think big than to think small. The study of personal development was the single most significant reason I've been able to have the success I have today. Personal development is like going to the gym. It doesn't work immediately, but if you continue exercising consistently, and continue to eat the proper foods, you won't even recognize yourself in one year. As I continued to pursue personal development and self-growth, the one common thread amongst all high achievers was they all set goals, were crystal clear on what they wanted, and they realized that failure was simply an ingredient for having massive success.

In the corporate world, as well as in school, we were taught that failure is bad. If you get an "F" in school, then you failed miserably. The philosophy in the Entrepreneurial world is much different. Failure simply means that you're on your way to a breakthrough in your business.

All the successful entrepreneurs that I've coached, and had as guests on my highly acclaimed iTunes podcast, *Success Hackers*, will tell you that they've failed many times. Failure gives us information so that we can make a course correction. When you're climbing your success mountain, you're going to run into roadblocks and speed bumps and maybe even setbacks. It's not whether or not you're going to encounter these; it's about how you're going to perceive them, and what you're going to do next.

You touched a little bit earlier on your why you do the things to help entrepreneurs but what drives you and gives you the passion for helping people that you help?

Scott Hansen: For a very long time, I was searching to find my purpose and what my passion was. Even though I had a successful sales career, I always knew that there was something missing. There was a time in my life when I struggled, and I didn't know what my purpose was, or what exactly it was that I wanted to create.

I was into personal development at a relatively young age. I was always listening to audios in hopes that one day I would find my passion and my purpose. Every day, I would spend hours in Barnes & Noble, reading autobiographies of super successful people; hoping that one day, I would find my purpose.

The reason I'm so passionate about helping other people is because I know what it's like to want so desperately to find your purpose, that you're willing to do just about anything to find it. When I get the opportunity to help people do the same, it's so amazing to see the proverbial "light switch" go on inside of people.

When these businesses come to you and these entrepreneurs, what is the most common obstacle preventing them from getting to the next level that they're trying to achieve the outcome you are describing.

Scott Hansen: The most common obstacle Entrepreneurs face is not having a plan, and feeling they have to be the lone wolf; doing everything by themselves. Most business owners spin a lot of plates but at the end of the day they're so busy at working in their business, they need help working on their business. I love what I do because every scenario is different. If someone wants to grow their business, sometimes it's a matter of hiring more people. When someone embarks upon the world of being an Entrepreneur, at first, they do everything in the business. They do the book-keeping, they do the sales, the marketing, customer service, etc. As the company grows, one of the hurdles that business owners have is being able to relinquish some of the responsibilities to other people.

Some are happy with being the solo-preneur; but if your goal is to build a growing, sustainable business, it's imperative to build a team around you.

I have a process called the 10/100/1000 principle.

This principle pertains to what types of activities a business owner should be focusing on.

Is the activity a $10/hour activity?
Is it a $100/hour activity?
Is it a $1,000/hour activity?

For ex: writing a blog post, spending hours per day posting on social media, creating an FB ad, or designing an opt-in page for your website, is a $10/hour activity. You can pay someone on FIVERR or ODESK $10 to do that activity for you.

As a business owner, the most valuable commodity you have is time.

The goal is to fill your schedule with $1000/hour activities, rather than spending your days focusing on activities that only produce a $10/hour result.

At this point, "letting go" and hiring a virtual assistant becomes a business owner's best friend.

A business owner's vision is to get clear on what the (3) most important Income Producing Activities, are, and spend 80% of your time on these activities to drive the lion's share of your revenue.

HAVING A PLAN

Think about it like this: have you ever hired a personal trainer? If the answer is yes, I'm assuming it was to help you get results quicker.

You're probably tired of going to the gym day after day, and not seeing the type of outcomes you wanted. This personal trainer's job is to get you in the best physical shape, in the quickest amount of time

You hired this personal trainer because he/she has been able to help others achieve amazing bodies, and you want those same results.

Working with a coach is the same.

My clients hire me because they've been trying for several years to grow their business, but they can't seem to get past a certain plateau, or "stick point".

A lot of times, they feel overworked, overwhelmed, and burnt out. Getting to the next level, although it sometimes involves learning new skill sets, primarily comes down to training your brain to think a different way. As someone that helps my clients become high achievers, I sit down and help them create an *Ultimate Success System* for themselves and their business through specific mindset and skill set strategies.

Can you describe to us how you've helped one of your clients, helped them succeed in overcoming some obstacles they came to you for help?

Scott Hansen: I once helped a business owner client of mine triple his revenue within six months. We first did that by getting crystal clear on what success looked like for him. We also developed a system of how he can get new client on a consistent basis. It's fun to have a vision of what your life/business would like to look like in three years, but the most important part of setting and achieving goals is what I like to call the "90 Day Focus". Research has been proven that our brains cannot focus on setting and achieving a goal past 90 days.

It's important to "chunk down" your goals into 90-day segments. The reason for this is you want to bite size goals on your way to the larger goals you've set for yourself.

For ex: let's say your goal is to add an extra $100k to your overall bottom line.

It's much easier for your brain to focus on $25k (every 90 days), rather than concentrate on the high goal of $100k. Once you know HOW to earn the $25k per 90 days, the likelihood you'll be able to earn more than that shortly becomes much greater.

90 days also allows you to achieve "wins" or "atta-boys" much quicker. Building confidence is one of the most important things you can do as an Entrepreneur. When you hit your 90-day goal of $25k, you have proven to yourself that $25k can be reached. All of us perform on a different level when we have confidence in ourselves to hit a particular goal.

For this particular client, once we designed the 90 Day Focus, then we set parameters. We looked at where he was focusing the majority of his time; the $10/100/1,000/ hour activity. We quickly found out that he was focusing most of his time on the $10/hour activity. Once we got clear on which tasks represented the $1000/hour activities (getting new clients), that's where we began to spend almost all of his time.

I also suggested that he raise his fees.

His biggest fear was, "if I raise my fees, what if I lose some of my current clients?"

I explained to him that, some of his current clients might not pay these higher fees, and actually might go with another vendor. But, I also knew that he was providing a solution to their problems, undercharging for his services and that the majority of new clients would indeed pay for his skill set. At first, he was apprehensive to do this, and it took a lot of convincing on my end. After finally committing to raising his fees, within six months, he was able to triple his revenue, while getting (3) new clients, charging more money for his services, and had a renewed confidence about his life and business.

That's a great example, thanks for sharing that with us. What's the most important thing that the reader should think about in growing their business, or getting over those obstacles of; "I can't afford to hire somebody else." What's the most important thing they should think of first?

Scott Hansen: Some people say, "Scott, what if I don't have the money to hire a coach?"

My answer is very straightforward. What scenario sounds better?

Scenario A)
- Doing it all by yourself and being the "one man band".
- Not having the ability to bounce ideas off other like-minded business owners.
- Spending tens of thousands of dollars on the newest, latest online course only to realize this isn't what matters to grow your business.
- Spending years "trying to figure this out".

Scenario B)
- Having a coach or a mentor to guide you every step of the way.
- Having this coach hold you accountable to your goals.
- Being able to bounce ideas off this coach.
- Celebrating your wins with this person.
- By having a coach, you cut the learning curve in half so that you can gain ground quickly and experience success.

Let's go back to the personal trainer example.

You've been going to the gym year after year, and not seeing the results you want, doesn't it make sense to try a different approach? If you knew how to get the body you wanted, wouldn't you already have it?

The cost of hiring a personal trainer is irrelevant.

If it costs me $5k to hire a personal trainer, and this expert could get me the body that I've never had, is it worth it?

OF COURSE!

It's the same thing for hiring a business/life/career/ coach.

If it costs you $5, $10, $20k to hire a business coach, and that business coach could help you generate an extra $100k in revenue, and help you achieve greater success in your life and business, was it worth it?

ABSOLUTELY!

Working with a coach has many benefits. They can keep you on track when the going gets tough. As Entrepreneurs, we are pushing the limits every day on what's possible for our business. With a coach, you have a straight set of eyes and ears. Their only goal is to help you get results and achieve the goals that you've set for yourself.

There's a reason the greatest athletes, influential CEOs, and the most successful Entrepreneurs have coaches. Each of these individuals strives to be world class in their respective fields. Their goal is to get the edge on their competition, and hiring a coach, allows them to see every angle.

Building a business, becoming an Entrepreneur, and pursuing your dreams, can be overwhelming and exhilarating all at the same time. It takes patience, an understanding support team, knowledge, faith, particular skill sets, and the right mindset.

If you want more money, more freedom, a bigger business, more success, or more influence, you will have to BECOME someone different.

Focus on being better today than you were yesterday. Turn off the TV, and start reading books on leadership, marketing, sales, personal growth.

Start surrounding yourself with people who are more successful, and further along than you.

Some people think that Success is this elusive thing available to the few amongst us. This couldn't be further from the truth. Success is attainable for everyone who has a strong desire, a no-quit attitude, and a commitment that's unshakeable.

I want to leave you with my favorite quote of all time from Theodore Roosevelt:

"It is not the critic who counts; not the man who points out how the strong man stumbles, or where the doer of deeds could have done them better. The credit belongs to the man who is actually in the arena, whose face is marred by dust and sweat and blood; who strives valiantly; who errs, who comes short again and again, because there is no effort without error and shortcoming; but who does actually strive to do the deeds; who knows great enthusiasms, the great devotions;   who   spends himself in a worthy cause; who at the best knows in the   end the triumph of high achievement, and who at the worst, if he fails, at least fails while daring greatly, so that his place shall never be with those cold and timid souls who neither know victory nor defeat."

Wishing You MASSIVE Success!

If somebody's ready to get started now, how can they find out more and how can they get connected? Can they email you or call you?

Scott Hansen: If someone wants to learn more about *Business Breakthrough* coaching program, best way to do that is to go to my email, which is **scott@scotthproductions.com** Also, make sure to check out one of the fastest growing podcasts for Entrepreneurs on iTunes, , *Success Hackers* (www.successhackers.net)

Perfect. Thank you very much.

WEBSITE:
www.scotthansenconsulting.com

EMAIL:
scott@scotthproductions.com

LINKEDIN:
https://www.linkedin.com/in/shansen1

FACEBOOK:
https://www.facebook.com/scott.hansen.7106

TWITTER:
https://twitter.com/scotthansen1210

PHONE:
(310) 254-0136

Leading Business Transformation Strategist

Slay Your Inner Dragon And Achieve Success

After working for 20 years in corporate life, juggling three young kids and family, changing career paths to try to find balance, Claudia realized her concept of "success" had changed. She came home one Friday evening, burnt out, exhausted and realized she had worked her entire career for other people's companies, to help them grow their businesses and often to the detriment of her personal well-being.

The epiphany that changed the direction of life happened one Friday evening in May while sitting at the open window as the breeze blew in the fresh earth smells unique to that beautiful season of rebirth. Claudia called her husband over and told him she wanted to STOP. And that's all she said and waited. Stop what exactly?

Most of us fantasize at times that we just want to leave the struggles behind, turn over a new page, start a new chapter, but then reality sets in and we settle, stay status-quo and only dream of things we believe are unattainable. Claudia didn't want to settle. With her husband and family behind her, she broke the golden handcuffs apart to reboot her career path and with conscience deliberation, changed her life.... the entrepreneurial journey began.

Seven years after Co-Founding Dig It Apparel Inc. and bootstrapping the ENTIRE time, her company entered Australia with their products and this little company she co-created became "International".

After striking a deal with Kevin O'Leary and appearing on the TV show Dragons' Den (the Canadian equivalent of the US' Shark Tank), she was asked to speak to organizations on the perspective of starting a business and striking a deal with Kevin. One connection led to another and shortly thereafter, Claudia was asked to speak at an entrepreneur's conference in front of 400 people. Walking out on the stage, knees shaking, she looked out at the largest audience since leaving her sales career behind. The room was quiet, all eyes turned to Claudia and she prayed her PowerPoint wouldn't lull them to sleep...then launched the talk. She started speaking from the heart about the fears and rewards about starting a business and leaving the corporate safety-net behind. She loved the feeling of being on stage, looking into the faces, watching people nod, making them laugh at stories and touching lives in a positive way. On that stage, an unexpected new chapter in her career was born. She again listened to her inner compass to move in a new direction. The words, "You love this...do this more. Do what you love!" filled her mind while coming off that stage.

This chapter is all about taking risks, listening to your inner voice, trusting in yourself to step across the chasm of fear that can hold us back and through an open door of abundant opportunity.

Conversation with Claudia Harvey

Claudia thanks for joining us again today. So tell us about your business and the types of customers you help.

Claudia Harvey: Well, I own a couple of businesses. Through the course of my career, I've obtained a variety of skills that enable me to diversify and assist entrepreneurs as well as companies catapult their success to a new level in sales, marketing and operations...I've worked in each of these areas extensively both in the private and public sectors.

I co-founded a business a few years ago called "Dig It Apparel" and the flagship product we created and designed is in retail stores across North America and Australia. In the infancy of our company, we went on a Canadian TV Show called Dragons' Den which is the equivalent of the business show Shark Tank in the US and as a matter of fact, one of the Sharks on the US based show, Kevin O'Leary, was a Dragon on Dragons' Den. Dig It struck a deal with Kevin, and that immediately validated our company and product idea and also provided us national exposure.

Since Dig It launched on national TV, companies and individuals approached me and asked me to speak to their organizations and help them with their own strategies. That developed into a speaking and consulting business. I enjoy motivational keynote speaking across North America to entrepreneurial organizations, women's groups, and private conferences...really anywhere where people want inspiration to turn their dreams into a reality and the insights in how to make that happen.

Perfect, so you described a couple of businesses. What led you to the field of you helping the other companies get unstuck and how did you get started in that?

Claudia Harvey: When the Dig It business aired in 2009 on Dragons' Den, it was a brand new start-up in its infancy. As of

2015, our products are in Canada, the United States and Australia. We started the business from scratch, with a limited budget and because it was necessary to be hands-on to grow it to where it is today, organizations came to me and asked me to speak on what it takes to launch a business, how to motivate yourself, how to make the leap and change your career in mid-stride to realize your dreams by becoming an entrepreneur. I heard the same questions repeated no matter what type of group I spoke to. People seemed to want to hear the answer to "how."

Though I had years of experience in sales, I perform the Operations role in Dig It and learned Operations in my corporate jobs. It can be very detailed and isolating at times. When I was asked to go onstage in front of people, I realized how much I missed it and thoroughly enjoy helping people. I think that was a critical factor that was missing in my life up to that point. I love connecting with others and inspiring them to reach their next level of personal success. And when they do, it's just so personally rewarding for me.

So everything that I've built up through my life and my career led to the point of being on stage and connecting with entrepreneurs, business people and women, and that in turn led me to the next phase of my career.

If I may, I'd like to add, that I seem to have found a niche with women and women's groups. Women appear to resonate with my story and I fell into helping women as a sideline to what I was doing. Because I had a corporate career and with three kids at home, made the conscious decision to leave corporate life behind, leave the 6-figure salary, all the trappings, and become an entrepreneur... that resonates with women. It's like, oh my goodness, so she did that, I could do that. And how did she do that? Well, I need to talk to her about how to do that. Because of my background and deliberately carving out my own path, I have been able help women find their path and to me that's just so positive. If I can positively influence their lives, they in turn affect those around them and the world becomes a better place!

Often I speak to individuals, women or men, and they need a gentle nudge or guidance to move their business forward. For instance, they may have a business idea and they have no idea how to get it off the ground. I've done that throughout my corporate career and of course through Dig It.

For the Start-up organization or person, I help them strategize, we plan, and I run them through how to launch their product or their service with success. Sometimes you don't know what you don't know and can waste valuable time, money and energy in false starts. I help them focus, turn their hopes to goals and then into reality.

And then I also help existing businesses grow in new directions. They could be in business for three years, five years, ten years, 17 years, etc. and they're stuck. They may want to re-energize their business, re-focus or often make more revenue and do not understand what's holding them back. It's a very similar process to start-ups but on a larger scale. It's very goal-driven and plan-oriented. The same strategies apply to each of those scenarios. It's planning: looking at your goals, moving backward from your ultimate goal in small incremental and steps, incorporating a marketing plan and financial plan to match the goals and projections and then breaking those down into bite size pieces. Reverse-engineering. Eventually, we get to a strategic and focused plan that everyone can envision, get behind and have the management team move in the same direction, motivated towards success. Knowing HOW to get to that outcome is 75% of the battle.

People have come to me and sought advice on how to start a business, but don't have any idea where to start. They may not even have an idea, but they do know they are not satisfied with their current lives and want some personal coaching. They are afraid of the risks involved to change but desire something else in their lives. I often suggest they can get their feet wet by joining a network marketing organization with a product or service they would want to personally use every day. Then they can begin to represent these products honestly. Often these organizations have strong leadership and support with an infrastructure in place to assist an individual to start a business. A person can start down this path without the necessity of leaving a current job and income. They can mitigate personal risk and still learn aspects of developing their own business. The upside can be so rewarding. You can make extra money, learn from people that have already become successful and want the same for you and obtain a sense of personal accomplishment, all the while enjoying tax right offs!

Perfect. Let's go into that a little bit. I'm sure a lot of the readers are at that point of transition in their life, but it's in the back of their mind. It's how do I get out of corporate and become an entrepreneur? What kind of tips can you give on that?

Claudia Harvey: First of all, do not be impulsive. That's critical. I see many people frustrated in their corporate job and who doesn't? You get frustrated in any job. It doesn't matter what job it is. Even when you're an entrepreneur, you can be frustrated. But don't be impulsive and just quit. Plan and determine a course of action to take, and then execute. When I decided to leave the corporate world, I had a small nest egg saved and a network of family and friends that was very supportive. Leaving the corporate life behind, I realized I would no longer have the big car allowance, the benefits and all the trappings that come with corporate life. So I planned for that. I made sure that I wasn't impulsively quitting just because I had a bad day. I desired to do something else in my life. Within a six month period of coming to the realization I wanted a change, my friend and now co-founder of Dig It introduced me to the idea of the unique product we then created. She was looking for a partner and I thought the opportunity was ripe for the taking. I became an entrepreneur and started something for myself, took all my gained experience and used it for me this time...not a company that would sap my strength and take my well-earned expertise.

Now this was a huge epiphany for me which I talk about to entrepreneurs...I had struggled, strived, desired to be successful in corporate life since I was ten years old and I finally reached what most people would say is "successful" in my corporate career, but when I got there, I realized all of these trappings, what I call the golden handcuffs, was not for me. Leaving that behind and becoming an entrepreneur was the first step to move my life into the direction of my choosing. It wasn't impulsive. I had a conscious understanding that starting a new business must have strategic plan and focus. You create a business plan, a marketing plan, and a financial plan that all work together. You understand that there could be a significant shift in your personal financial stability, and there may be lean times. You need to accept that possibility in your lifestyle. A lot of people jump into a business and waste so much money because they don't have the planning.

I often encourage new entrepreneurs to revisit their goals every six months both personally and in business. Ask themselves the personal question if what they're doing is right for them and what can I change/should I change to help me achieve my ultimate goals? Same goes for the business objectives, often revisit the plan to achieve the goals that you set out early on. There is no "right" answer... We need to carve our own path and seek out guidance when we need it.

Those are great points. I always like this question when I speak to entrepreneurs. Along the way, entrepreneurs read a lot of books. Is there a book that you recommend or influenced you along the way?

Claudia Harvey: Yes. Napoleon Hill's Think and Grow Rich. I think I've read it five times, and I have it in the audio book as well. One of my favorite quotes is "Desire is the starting point of all achievement, not a hope, not a wish, but a keen pulsating desire which transcends everything." Which I think can resonate with many entrepreneurs and business owners. I enjoyed it the first time I read it, and there are so many nuggets in that book that I re-read it again and again. Sometimes I put it on audio in certain sections and hear it again. I also read the book, what to Say When You Talk to Yourself by Shad Helmstetter early in my career. It helped me with putting life in perspective and keeping the negative thoughts at bay that can creep in. But here's a little secret, I enjoy reading fiction as well. It's an escape in my mind, a movie in my head.

Yeah. It's an excellent book. What about a person? Has someone stood out along the way that's inspired you?

Claudia Harvey: I'm going to give you a very personal answer. My Mom was the person that inspired me to who I am today. My parents were German immigrants, and they came over to North America in the post-war era. They were much, much older and in their 40's when they had my brother and I. And very similar to today's immigrants, my Mom didn't know the language, came to the new world and needed to incorporate new social expectations into her routine. When she was in her 50's, she and my father started a hairdressing salon in the small city where I lived just outside of Toronto. And she did that until she was 70. In reflecting back upon her with my adult eyes, I see how my mother changed her life numerous times, overcame challenges and fears and quietly instilled that confidence in her children as part of our world growing up. She was always a person that was optimistic, happy, looked at the positive things in life, and I think that came from her background and where she came from which was post-war Germany. She was a child of the depression era and instead of having her experiences jade her, without a doubt she always, always looked for the positive things in life. If it was a rainy day, she'd say, well the plants need it she never complained. Personally, I cannot stand drama in my life, and she instilled these qualities in me. If she had been born in a different era, if she had been born today, she would've been a powerhouse. She was just amazing and I'm sure there are many stories out there of other fabulous, stoic women that just put their head down and did what they had to do...and impacted those around them with light and laughter.

Well, that's an incredible story. Thanks for sharing that. That's a great example that it's never too late to start.

Claudia Harvey: Yeah, she was quietly, inspirationally wonderful. I want to be her when I grow up. That's what I tell everybody.

I just got the chills. Yes. Absolutely. So I guess that leads to my next question about what drives you and gives you the passion for helping the people that you help. I think you answered that in this last question. But if you want to expound on that a little bit, by all means.

Claudia Harvey: In my life, I always strive to have three things in my life, and that's strength, balance, and harmony. Strength from within and I surround myself with people that will support me, are like-minded, are optimistic. Balance means that I can manage both my personal goals and business objectives with the wheels staying on the cart...that can certainly take some maneuvering at times! Harmony occurs when the people that matter in my life are all moving together in harmony. And each of us is in congruence with our personal goals and supporting each other. And if those 3 things are not in my life, then I'm out of synch. It affects how I move through life. In retrospect, I realize that as I added family and other commitments outside a career to my life, I inherently gravitated towards these words until I carved out an individual path that worked for me. And I think a lot of entrepreneurs and business people strive for the similar things, but they might not even know it or have yet to identify it in themselves.

The readers have common misconceptions. So what would be the biggest misconception about them achieving, you know, crossing over from being corporate to transitioning to an entrepreneur and being the captain of their ship, so to speak? What would be the biggest misconception that you have experienced?

Claudia Harvey: I think a lot of business people or entrepreneurs when they're crossing over , believe it's going to be easy, that they're going to have flexibility in their schedule, they're going to make more money than they currently do..... And often that's not the immediate reality. This realization can hit a newly minted entrepreneur in the face and then fears of failure set in. Those fears can be internalized and taken personally, and often planning could mitigate it and the key to expectations. To reach personal and business goals, you need to have inner focus, drive, and the determination that's driven by YOU. It's going back to planning the HOW to get there and working towards that with focus.

And when I say the drive must come from within, this often becomes very apparent a few months into a new venture. As a startup, you don't have one job. You often do everything. You have to be sales; customer service, accounts receivable, billing, logistics, everything. And a lot of people don't understand that in the lifestyle of a small business you are a jack of all trades, do not have subject matter experts to call on when you are stumped, and it can be very isolating. Often, they think that they can make money immediately out of the gate without realizing the expenses that may come up. And when they don't make instant money, they quit. It can be hard, and a lot of people quit when it's hard. If it were easy, everyone would do it. Success comes with tenacity, focus and drive. On the upside, when you reach some success, that success is yours, and that feeling is intoxicating! You wake up at 3 in the morning because you have this incredible epiphany, and have to deal with it right now because it's driving you forward. It's your a passion. The more passionate you are about what you do, the easier it is to view "hurdles" as stepping stones and just something new to learn on the journey. You're mindset shifts when you find your passion and things will start to fall in line. So if you can figure out what your passion is, the how will unfold.

How do you feel about, you talked about people getting to a certain point, and then they quit? As far as mindset, do you help clients with that so they can overcome those challenges?

Claudia Harvey: That's one thing a lot of entrepreneurs and people have in common, and I enjoy helping them overcoming their personal limiting beliefs and positively impacting their mindset. Mindset is crucial to being an entrepreneur, businessperson and succeeding in any profession because mindset directly relates to communication style. Communication style relates to how you sell yourself, your business and services. If you believe in yourself and your business and that belief is embedded in your core, that feeling will come across when you communicate. And if you cannot or do not sell yourself well, your mindset is not in-line with your desired outcomes. If you do not believe you will succeed, you are already starting off with a sabotaging thought that will directly relate to how you perform. Communication is crucial in all aspects of your life: your planning, selling yourself and increasing revenue. So many of people come to me and say, "Oh, I have salespeople. I don't sell." And I point out that everyone needs to sell. You need to sell your vision to your salespeople and your salespeople understand that the captain is driving the ship. They get motivated by you; that message comes from the top down, and they, then, go out to the marketplace to communicate your message and brand. And when people say, "I don't like sales, I'm not very good at sales" we have to change that mindset. Everyone has unique experiences that we can draw upon and sets us apart and you have something that the world needs to hear about. I help them draw that out and they start to understand that there are qualities in each of us that we can leverage off of which then affects communication and leads to an upward spiral of success. For example, I was speaking at a woman's conference, and a young woman came up to me afterwards and told me she was an engineer. She completely undervalued herself in her conversation with me. I know how difficult it is to become an engineer AND it's still a very male dominated industry. She said she was thinking of leaving the profession and felt she wasn't very good at it. I asked her, "Do you believe that you have succeeded in certain aspects of your life?" And she said no, that she wasn't succeeding very well at all. I pointed out to her that she went into a male-dominated profession that's tough to graduate from. Number one, she got in. Number two, she graduated. Number three, she has a job in engineering. So she could take all of that experience and background unique to her and use it to "re-engineer" her life to what she wants to do. She needs the vision and the belief she does have something to offer. A lot of people don't realize how much they have in their personal background they can leverage off of. And that's what I help them identify so they can utilize it and feel good about themselves. And then their small tiny steps become a huge upward spiral of success. The little increments of success build upon other success and then the doorways just open up.

That leads us then to the next question about how you've taken somebody from their challenges and got them across the line and overcome their obstacles. Could you tell us a short story about a client you have helped?

Claudia Harvey: I've also worked with companies that have been in business for years led by the same people and they are stuck. They just don't know what they want. They've lost cohesion and focus. They no longer know where they want to take their business and are fractured. For example, a couple of partners might want to leave or want to go in an opposing direction. Some may want to increase their product offerings. Others might wish to remain status quo. So I bring them all together to realign their goals. We determine a 3, 5, 10-year plan. So we get everybody on the same page, and identify what has to happen to reach those particular goals, and we have to identify what those goals might be. We also identify who is responsible for the assigned tasks so there is accountability. We realign and moving them in the same direction.

If you had one piece of advice to give somebody, what would it be? If it's considering transitioning from starting up their own business or being an entrepreneur, what would that advice be?

Claudia Harvey: One word that always comes to mind when I'm asked that question is the word choice. You have a choice in everything that you do in life. You have a choice to turn off the TV and play with your kids. You have a choice to read the next business book that might advance your ideas. You have a choice to identify you want to change your life and start moving in a direction. You have a choice to go to a networking function because you never know who you may meet that could change your life. Everybody has a choice in life and when they say that, I'm stuck in my job, I don't believe that. It might take a person awhile to move your life in a different direction and you have choices you can make to leave that job one day. Overcome the hurdles and fear so you can move forward with incremental steps towards something that drives you or, choose to stay in the same place. If you stay, before you know it, years have passed, and that wish for a change is all that it ever was… just a wish. Turn the dream into a goal and into an achievement. Determine what's relevant to your life and what you need to do to move towards it. Are there sacrifices to be made and are you willing to do them to follow your path? Everything in life is a choice. It might take you a while to get there, but you have a choice to change your life if you don't like the life you're living.

If somebody's ready to get started, how could they find out more about how they could work with you or find out more information?

Claudia Harvey: Really simple. It's claudiaharvey.com. So that's my website. And my email address is charvey@claudiaharvey.com.

Thank you for sharing all those awesome nuggets and I really appreciate it.

Claudia Harvey: Oh, my pleasure.

WEBSITE:
www.ClaudiaHarvey.com

EMAIL:
claudiaharvey@rogers.com

TWITTER:
@CharveyBiz

LINKEDIN:
https://ca.linkedin.com/in/claudiaharvey

FACEBOOK:
https://www.facebook.com/ClaudiaHarveyConsulting

YouTube:
http://bit.ly/1X11KWq

SKYPE:
Claudia.Harvey4101

PHONE:
(416) 419-5731

International Staffing Professional & Business Owner

Turning Your Reactive Job Search into a Proactive Job Search

When C.J. was ten years old, he realized that selling subscriptions to the Chicago Tribune made him five times the amount of money versus delivering the paper. So he paid someone to run his routes on the weekend so that he could sell subscriptions.

C. J. realized early on that there wasn't one way to do anything, only different ways. Ironically it was High School and his focus, or lack thereof, on academics. He barely graduated High School and chose to focus his attention on opening businesses and working. Lack of concentration on academics resulted in a D- overall GPA. As a high school graduate, he didn't think he would be able to cut it in college, so he joined the military. Upon completing his military service, C.J. entered college and graduated with honors and made the dean's list. He realized that a lack of focus in one area, at one point in time, doesn't necessarily result in failure, especially if you have not followed the traditional path to success. He ultimately found that you could make your way as long as you had that focus to begin with and applied it when needed.

C.J.'s early attempts at entrepreneurship ended in disaster. It has been said many times, and he will merely reiterate what a multitude of entrepreneurs already know; fail early and fail often.

C.J. credits his success to not only hard work and taking advantage of the right opportunities but also the support he has received throughout his life. He could not have become the man, son, entrepreneur and father that he has become without his wife Lorna and his mother's example of strength and courage early on in C.J.'s life. His sense of adventure and taste for world travel came from his time in the military and the stories that his Grandfather, Jack Karnis, told him. He was his mentor and made C.J. the business man that he is today. And finally his four children, Kaelynn, Kiera, Connor and Ava. The inspiration that keeps him on track and focused. This has been C.J.'s recipe for success.

Conversation with CJ Seestadt

All right. Let's get right into it, CJ. Thanks for joining us today for this interview. So tell me about your business and the types of customers that you help.

CJ Seestadt: My business is a boutique executive search firm, as I mentioned. It is US veteran run and a minority-owned company that specializes in two things, the first being an executive search firm that engages in searches for the entire C-suite of executives (CEO's COO's CFO's). Our niche is that we specialize in confidential searches. In other words we help companies where a contentious environment exists among their leadership team and we work with company boards and owners to find the necessary leadership required to run their companies effectively. We place director level positions and up in the Chicago market and we're very Chicago market-centric in the sense that this is where we are based. We know the market better than most. And we are, because of the current economic state of Illinois and its budget impasse and $200 Billion dollars plus deficit, operating in a tenuous business environment. For these reasons the merger and acquisition market has exploded in Illinois. There is a lot of medium-sized, privately owned Mom and Pop companies in this market that have been family-owned, sometimes multi-generationally. They've had enough with the taxes and sometimes with just running the companies, and they're selling off in record numbers to national and international investors for $.50 to $75 on the dollar. So what you're seeing here in Illinois and primarily in Cook County is a change in dynamic within these family-owned businesses where the owners knew the employees and understood everything about the day to day operations, particularly in the manufacturing sector here, or what's left of it. You are seeing the company go from a family-owned business and evolving very quickly into an impersonal asset in a portfolio for an investment company. And you get everything that goes along with that, particularly the change in leadership, and that's where we're helping to not only transition leaders into these roles, but coach them along and assist the new C-level folks to understand the culture that we're parachuting them into.

The types of clients that you help are the C-level executives and the leaders that fall out of these acquisitions that maybe have to get another job or do something different?

CJ Seestadt: No, we're more on the opportunity side where we're filling the leadership positions in this market as mentioned earlier, we have two components of what we do and why my company, Advance Search International, is different. The first element is we're Chicago-centric, and we fill many leadership roles here. The second component is that we identify positions in developing and emerging countries, like the BRIC countries, for professionals who are 55 + years of age and that are struggling to find their next leadership role. As mentioned earlier, the two highest demographics for unemployment, per capita, in the Chicago-land area for adults are recent college graduates and professionals 55 years of age and older. There is a demand by national companies that have done very well in their respective country, and they've just made it to the international stage. And they're looking for American business professionals with the business acumen to be the face of their company internationally. We've got an office in Shanghai, China with plans to open an office in Mexico City in 2016 and Sao Paulo, Brazil or Bogota, Colombia in 2017. In China, there's a demand right now for the manufacturing industry specifically. Unfortunately, there is a surplus of very talented professionals who are in their 50's and 60's, and they are looking for that next challenge. Generally speaking, the older candidates we speak with that are 55 years of age and older tend to be empty nesters with adult children that have downsized and tend to live in a smaller home or condominium. Older candidates are positioned at a point in their life to take advantage of an opportunity internationally. That is what we do, and that is how we help those that need it most.

Interesting.

CJ Seestadt: To the best of my knowledge, we're the only company that does this.

I like how you said that the people you target tend to have adult kids and they're able to grasp an opportunity. I always refer to that as I'm living my third life.

CJ Seestadt: Right.

I had the military life, I raised my kids, and I'm still relatively young, and you can take opportunities like that. That's an awesome service. So what led you to this field and how did you get started in it?

CJ Seestadt: Oh, what led me to do this? What leads anybody anywhere?

Either life is disrupted or a tragedy.

CJ Seestadt: Right. "Life is what happens while you are busy making other plans". Isn't that what John Lennon said?

Right.

CJ Seestadt: So what led me here? Obviously, my background is diverse, as diverse as most entrepreneurs, from a former professional soccer player in Europe to working in broadcasting for ABC and CNN International, to opening my own business in

Scotland. But for the past several years I have worked in staffing as a COO for an international staffing company based out of India. Given my vast and varied experiences in several industries and my C-level experience, I can work very effectively in the Executive Search world. I was allowed to work as an "Intrepreneur" in many roles. In other words, I was authorized to be an entrepreneur within a structured organization, that was not my own. Entrepreneurial types are what companies are looking for today, and this is what I coach to my candidates and try to emphasize to individuals who are 55 + who are in the job market. Given the current job market, specifically here in Chicago, there was an apparent demand or need for what we evolved into at Advanced Search International, Inc... So really, it was looking at trends that were occurring and where the future was going because executive search is nothing new. There are loads of companies out there doing it. How do you differentiate yourself? I tend to develop a superb rapport with the executives I work with because I used to be one. I have held leadership roles and opened companies most of my working life. I know what it's like to delegate, manage and multi-task. I can empathize with the day to day demands that not only my clients but my candidates must face.

You are a military veteran and you got some of that experience by being in the military, correct?

CJ Seestadt: I was in the military. That was my first career out of high school, the Naval Air Force. And that set the stage and gave me an excellent foundation for many things. And what did we learn in the Navy, Tracy? "Manage your time...?

Yes. Military success is about how to manage time. Lives depend on how well you dealt with that and this was a large part of our training.

CJ Seestadt: Or It will manage you!" Time management, I was taught that at a very early age and I would attribute that as one of the top three things that have made me a successful person

Absolutely.

CJ Seestadt: And I have the military to thank for that, as well as shaving every day.

Yes, I posted on Facebook yesterday that the most useful training tool we used to train recruits was the stencil card. You remember the stencil card?

CJ Seestadt: Yes, how can I forget? I still have an indentation on my index finger from that stencil pen. So yes, I do, Sir. Only at Great Lakes because Orlando and San Diego got their names embroidered on their government issued clothing and delivered.

If you couldn't master that, how could we possibly trust you with anything else? Where are your offices located?

CJ Seestadt: I am the Managing Director of Advanced Search International, Inc. We've got three offices; one in Shanghai, China and two in Illinois in Chicago and Hoffman Estates.

Of all the entrepreneurs that I'm privileged to talk to and interview, they always refer to a book that inspired them or helped them along the way. Is there one that stands out with you?

CJ Seestadt: Well, there are several. I mean, you know, I was a *Rich Dad, Poor Dad* aficionado. But the game changer for me was *Good to Great* by Jim Collins. "Get the right people on the bus."

How about a person or an individual along the way that really stands out that helped mold you?

CJ Seestadt: That's very easy. My grandfather, Jack Karnis. He's credited with co-inventing the corn dog. But it was known as the Pronto Pup then. He was one of the most influential people in my life and he, just like most grandfathers, left me with enough words of wisdom and anecdotes to fill this book. He was a farm boy from the U.P. of Michigan who served in World War II and everything that came with it; good, bad, ugly, indifferent. I learned a hell of a lot from him.

Great! We talked earlier about some things that help you do what you do, but deep down, what is your passion to do what you do to assist the people that you help?

CJ Seestadt: For most people, it's always easy to say "I help people" you know. I have a servant's heart. To say that I "help people" is a vanilla answer. It's how you help people. One of many things that I do to help people is that I try to share the passions that I've had in my life and find people who need help in identifying their passions. For example, utilizing my experience to help them build their businesses, their companies. But helping them through coaching, guiding, and teaching.

The people that you're helping, I mean once you're at an age of 55, You're towards the end of your supposed career or working career. I mean most probably have ten more good years if not more.

CJ Seestadt: I'm 46. So I am not quite there yet. I was recently told that the concept of retirement, as we know it today, will go the way of the dinosaur. Millennials will work towards an acceptable standard of living but most will not retire as we know it.

So that's a pretty traumatic point in somebody's life. I've lived that, and I didn't experience it until I got out of the military but experienced the corporate thing, so I could just imagine, and I was only in corporate America 7 years. Spending 20 years and then saying, hey, we don't need you anymore or we're downsizing or whatever the situation is has to be difficult. Do you find that they're more apt to become entrepreneurs at that point or do they still want to enter the marketplace and assume a position of leadership?

CJ Seestadt: Well, going back to my grandfather, one of the things he used to say was "entrepreneurs were born, not made." Now, how much of that is true, Nature or nurture? I don't know. But I do believe different personality types work better in an entrepreneurial environment as opposed to the office culture. There are those who find comfort in the military or very structured environments like corporate America, and those who fear and dread every day of the unknown and those who don't. I'm going to quote my friend, Andy, who is also an entrepreneur and printing business owner. 'The thing that I love and hate about being an entrepreneur is the same thing, and that is not knowing what's going to happen tomorrow.' I think there are just a lot of people who do not cope well with uncertainty. Can they become an entrepreneur? Sure, anyone can. America is about that. Are you wired to be an entrepreneur? It doesn't take too long to figure that out.

You have all these executives and experts that are in corporate America, and they're being dumped out into society. So it almost becomes survival of the fittest. Do I become an entrepreneur? Do I get another job? So what is the percentage of

41

people that are becoming entrepreneurs or do you even have any idea?

CJ Seestadt: The numbers in Chicago for unemployed people 55 and over being are between 4.1 to 4.7 percent per market, and that is not a terrible statistic given the national rate is 5.7% but older workers who do lose a job spend longer periods out of work, and if they do find another job, it tends to pay less than the one they left. The alarming thing is that it is the fastest growing demographic of unemployed people, per capita, in most markets. The natural evolution is that someone got fired after the crash in 2008. We saw the largest mass firings and layoffs since The Great Depression. So what happened was that you had a bunch of, and I'm using my quote, end quote fingers right now, "experts" who were an expert of whatever they specifically did at their company, and they were big companies; Kraft, PepsiCo, United Airlines, etc. And after they were let go, they became "consultants", and I'm doing the finger thing again. This was not just in Chicago but across America, these "experts" went out, and they were good at that one thing that they did at their company, but they couldn't grasp as a whole how to consult business owners in areas outside of their sphere of knowledge let alone run a business. Or identifying what the big problem was and how to attack it from different angles. When starting out, most successful people can reach out to their network and get one or two clients that will sustain things and even grow your revenue and then bam, they lose one. That's where their lack of experience in marketing or business development starts the tailspin, if they don't have specific knowledge in that area. They can't sustain a client base or build new business. This was usually the beginning of the end. They knew how to do something and one thing well. Some people are an amazing chef or a great barber with many customers working in a structured environment, and they want to open a restaurant or their shop, and they fail not because they aren't exceptional at what they do but that they don't know how to run a business, which is a different animal. So what that led to was what we called here in the Chicago market, "consultant fatigue". Businesses hiring these people who were either close personal friends or recommendations and referrals they were good but didn't fix the problem and were paid a lot of money. This led to many companies in this market going back to the large consulting companies again. And that is where we find ourselves today. Everything kind of reset itself.

Interesting. What do you find to be the biggest misconception when somebody's downsized, or they're at an age of, you know, 55 or older of achieving or finding a new opportunity?

CJ Seestadt: Well, that's a great question, because the highest rate of unemployed people, per capita, in the US is recent college grads. The reason is, simply put, that while you're in college, they tell you that you're going to get a job, until you're out of college and you can't. And that's the real issue. I don't think people get as pro-active on their job search when they should, and this is what I tell college students now when I speak on campus, start your job search now. I don't care what year of college you are in. You start it now. The majority of them are waiting until they get that diploma and they go and talk to career services or Mom and Dad or whatever. But that's not enough. Older professionals fall into that same trap. Whether you're a director or an executive, and you know that you will be transitioning out soon you need to start looking while you are still employed. The beginning of the out-boarding process starts with your company sending you to a career coach, and those people get paid to tell you that you're going to be fine, you'll find jobs. Here are some job leads, and these older professionals believe they will get a new job without a problem as they are being told that until six months have passed and they are sitting at home after they have exhausted their network and resources and feel that there is no way forward. My advice to those still working is "stay employed for as long as you can". When you're a passive (employed) candidate, this is where you're most lethal. That position is your best opportunity to find a job. Don't tell anyone you're transitioning out. When you are interviewing, tell them that you're exploring opportunities and not transitioning out, and it changes the whole dynamic because there are plenty of active (Unemployed) candidates out there. People want to hire passive, relevant candidates. Companies WILL hire them.

Yes, I just read that 95% of the job or employment opportunities are non-published.

CJ Seestadt: 70% are never advertised and passed on by word of mouth mostly. 30% are, and of that, only 2% to 3% of those are filled with online searches and job boards.

Usually, if it's reached a point that the position hasn't been filled, it's...

CJ Seestadt: Not a good job.

Yes, you're getting the crumbs. That's amazing how that works. So, I mean entrepreneurs think a little bit differently than people that have jobs. Do you find that people at that point, have they invested in self-development or mindset training or is that like non-existent?

CJ Seestadt: Sometimes but generally speaking, only if the company's made them and about what they had to do professionally. I think that is why this C-level coaching culture is thriving and growing. It's larger than I've ever seen it. When I go to networking events, there are a lot of executive coaches. Don't get me wrong, coaching is powerful. I mean I believe in coaching, and I always refer to major league baseball. These guys are the best in the world at their craft, and they need two things. They need to go back to fundamentals every spring, and revisit fundamentals and they need coaches. So I'm all about coaching, but there seem to be a plethora of choices and styles regarding how one should be coached at the executive level and very little consistency regarding methodology. Are they taking the time to develop themselves and their soft skills, as opposed to just focusing on their hard skills and their business acumen? No, but they're addressing the need to. And that is a start.

Can you describe how you can help someone overcome those challenges and get the end results that they are looking for?

CJ Seestadt: It comes down to understanding the playing field. Case in point, many people don't realize that 70% of jobs aren't advertised. Secondly, they don't understand the real power of their network. Many of these executives that I work with are too proud to ask peers, friends and family for job leads. Finding a new career is a numbers game so why wouldn't you? It comes down to educating people on the proper way to execute a proactive job search as opposed to the traditional reactive job search that everyone has grown accustomed to. A reactive job search is not very efficient or effective and provides very few results.

Is there an example of someone that you could talk about that you've helped?

CJ Seestadt: I could give you many because, as I had mentioned earlier, I have become the career doctor or career lawyer of my entire circle. When someone I know has a friend or family member that is in transition or has just been terminated, I get the call. So every day, and I mean that, every day, I'm giving someone that's just been fired, and it's particularly folks 55 and over, advice on how to become a successful job seeker. For example, yesterday, I spoke with a chief marketing officer who had been with the same firm for 22 years, and he was let go at the ripe old age of 53 and had no idea where he was going to go. He came to me with his "resume" and "I don't want to bother my friends or family. I'm embarrassed enough that they don't know I'm not employed anymore. So I have been online to see what's available, and then just send my resume to them." I hear this a lot. Sending your resume out to your immediate network is a very natural response to being fired and this was this gentleman's exact plan. The advice I gave him is the advice I give everyone, and that is first and foremost, you never have one resume.

Great piece of advice right there.

CJ Seestadt: Going from reactive to proactive means writing a resume for every position and this is very straightforward. They give you the answers to the test in the job description. Most employers use word filtering software to weed out candidates instead of physically reading each resume because they receive so many; it is best that you incorporate every skill set you see in that job description into the resume that you use to apply for that specific position. And then you don't submit it through their system unless they ask you to. You then use your resources, primarily LinkedIn, to find out if you can have your resume hand-delivered. Now taking a step back, you want to identify companies you wish to work for and with. That's proactive. You want to find 20 companies, and if you're working somewhere, like this gentleman was for 22 years, you know that you've worked on a project with some companies and thought "hey, this is a cool company." or "wow, if there was an opportunity at this place, I'd go to work there now." Knowing that 70% of the jobs aren't advertised, start looking at your connections, make some phone calls, and go out for some informative luncheons at these companies if you can still reach out to your contacts there. I always recommend people to connect with the person in the office who always knows what is going on (you know the one) because they'll tell you all you need to know and it'll only cost you one lunch. And the power of the information they'll share with you will be invaluable and, in most times, will lead to an opportunity that you were not aware of. You submit your resume, but you make sure it's done on a personal level. And then from there, follow up, follow up, follow up. And people always say, "But I don't want to seem desperate or to bother anybody." Unless people come from a sales background or a marketing background, they tend not to follow up. They don't want to appear bothersome to people. And I always turn that around on them and say, "You were an executive, and we all tend to live and die by our task lists. How many times did somebody call you and you were thankful that they reminded you that they were there or reminded you of something that you had forgotten that was important?" And it only takes about three days, on average, for any one thing to fall off your task list. So the folks that are hiring are appreciative when you call them and keep following up. There will be the occasional nasty one, but you're looking for a job. Get over it. Most people will be grateful that you reminded them because they have an open position. If you are qualified for that position. You're fixing a problem for them, and you're checking something off their task list. This is a big "aha" moment for the executives. So that's the process. That's what I talk my clients through. Does that help? So in summary, you have a resume for every position that you apply for. The secret is that the job description gives you the "answers to the test" so to speak. You must interject as many words from the job description into your resume before submitting it to the open position. Interjecting as many words from the job description is the second step to becoming a proactive job seeker. The first is going out and identifying 20 companies that you would want to work for and then identifying at least 8 to 10 positions that are not advertised, as previously mentioned 70% are not, by reaching out to your network and just asking people that work for or have ties to these companies. LinkedIn.com is an incredible tool, and not many people know how to utilize it effectively. That is where I can help.

Oh yes, perfect. The readers will definitely be able to connect with that, so thanks for sharing that. If somebody is ready or in a position that you described, how can they find out more about working with you?

CJ Seestadt: Gifts. I respond very well to gifts. Gifts, expensive luncheons, trips, the more exotic, the better. But no, do you want contact information?

Yes, it would be a good time to put that in here.

CJ Seestadt: My email address is cjs@asichicago.us, also you can reach out by phone (312) 646-5020. I am always happy to help in any way that I can. You'll find that we don't have a strong online presence, and that's by design. We specialize in confidential searches.

WEBSITE:
www.advancesearchinternational.com.

EMAIL:
cjs@asichicago.us

LINKEDIN:
https://www.linkedin.com/in/cj-seestadt-b99882

FACEBOOK:
https://www.facebook.com/cseestadt

Phone:
(312) 646-5020

Webb Financial Group

Helping Start-Ups, Businesses, and Individuals Get the Insurance Coverage They Need

Chris got his start selling coffee service to businesses in college.

His dad has been an entrepreneur for 50 years and always encouraged him to work for himself so he would be able to control his time and income potential.

When he understood that, the more he developed personally, the better he was able to serve his clients.

Chris knows it's all about adding value be it with his service or strategic introductions.

He remembers when he went from being a salesperson to a business owner signing his first lease and had to get a payroll service. Managing employees, making payroll, letting someone go that wasn't a cultural fit. He says all these things have helped me grow as a person and enabled me to gain the respect of the businesses and executives we work alongside.

It's all about the client, Chris says, listening to what is important to the customers, not trying to put their situation in a box.

Developing long term relationships and spending time with clients outside the office, that is when the trust really starts to develop.

When a person or company works with Chris and his team, they'll be covered.

Conversation with Chris Webb

Chris. Thanks for joining us today to be a part of this Success Hackers project. Tell us about your business and what types of customers you help.

Chris Webb: We work all aspects of insurance with individuals and small to medium size companies with our largest client being around 300 employees. We work in a broad cross-section of industries. We are not just industry specific. We also like start-up companies so we can grow with them, hopefully. We are doing employee benefits, business insurance, cyber liability coverage, workers comp, life insurance, long term disability, long term care; the full range of the programs for the business as well as the executives in the company.

Just so I am clear are you servicing solo-premiums or is there a particular corporation, as far as income that you work with or how does that work?

Chris Webb: We work with a lot of start-up companies. I mean, of course, the hi-tech start-up area in Chicago is very active, and there are lots of companies that we've seen that have gone from 5 or 10 employees to 200 employees in a pretty short period, a couple in just 2 to 3 years. We try to meet as many start-up companies as we can and cross our fingers at some of the ones that we have the privilege to do business with will have that kind of explosive growth. We'd like to ride the comet with them. We will work with anybody that needs help that is open to letting us evaluate the situation and giving them some expert help. Any person that needs individual health insurance or somebody that's starting a company and needs to get some basic business programs in place, we can help them out in any respect.

I like that comment, "ride the tail of the comet on the way up". So how did you get into this field and how did you get started in this business?

Chris Webb: I moved to Chicago in 1989. I was into golf then, and I'm still into golf. I played golf in college, and I was working in the golf industry in Florida. I met a woman down there who had graduated from law school up in Chicago, and I always wanted to live in this big city. I moved up here and got a job, not originally in insurance, but in sales. I ran into somebody that I had played golf with in college selling long-distance services for MCI at that time. It was a very commodity type of sale. It wasn't a relationship kind of situation where you're building a long-term relationship with clients. This guy told me he was in the insurance business, and there was also the competitive golf connection among his fellow office workers. So I was attracted to that and was attracted to the idea that I was going to be able to build up long-term relationships with people in an industry that is sales and relationship-based. I jumped at the idea, and that was in January '91 when I started the business, I worked for a couple of bigger agencies for the first, I guess 17 years in the business. I went off on my own eight years ago because I wanted to be independent, not representing just one insurance company. I wanted to have the flexibility and the freedom to try to find the exact, right program for the client that I'm talking to meet their particular needs. So it's been great being independent. I've evolved over the years into expanding lines to include commercial business insurance practices with a highly seasoned commercial line professional. I was a Life and Health guy since '91 but wanted to represent everything that clients ask to include in their portfolio, thus the property casualty business. I wanted to diversify my business with the concept that the Affordable Care Act could play with the revenue to the Employee Benefits side. The sectors of activity are often the entrée into the small business and then when that is well done, there are often other opportunities in the other lines. This is the way to get your foot in the door with the company and then ultimately be able to earn the right to talk to them about other areas of coverage, such as Employee Benefits or Life Insurance, which they might need.

You mentioned MCI being a commodity-type product and then you went into a relationship. And being in the insurance business, of course, it's based on relationships. I mean how is that different from you and the bigger companies? What are you providing?

Chris Webb: Well, I think insurance, in general, is about the relationship; there are a lot of people that aren't independent that still have deep relationships with their clients. Don't get me wrong, but there's also some big outfits out there around the country that are backed by private equity firms turning the little guy's head; there may be a relationship at the beginning, but then it gets lost in the shuffle of not meeting with the clients anymore. It's a shiny, new object and it turns a lot of people's heads, and they'll jump on the bandwagon, but then six months in, every time they call the 800 number, they're talking to a different person. No wonder there's no continuity regarding the relationship there; nobody knows the back-story, and that's kind of what we bring to the table. We know the people. At Webb, we have nine employees here with several on each platform of the insurance lines. We have an experienced group of people here, and so we're able to know the account, understand the dynamics, and the back-story on reports over time and grow with them. I think customers like the continuity in that; they like to be able to develop these relationships and know that someone will be in their corner speaking on their behalf in an industry that changes lingo daily. I believe they trust us for the long term and not just some random person on an 800 number.

Perfect. Yeah, that's kind of back to the old school way of doing business. I remember growing up when I was a kid that the insurance guy was at the house, we were breaking bread with them, we had relationships. So yeah, that's awesome. So this next question, every entrepreneur or business person I talk to has been influenced by a book they read or something that's, maybe even a movie. I know we spoke about this earlier, but could you go into a little bit about what's influenced you as far as books and things like that?

Chris Webb: Years ago, and now, my dad was a big influence on me. He had me take the Dale Carnegie course right after I got out of college. I was down in Florida. I was playing professional golf in the mini tour, kind of like the minor leagues of professional golf, in the late '80's. I took the Dale Carnegie course. I read several of his books, *How to Win Friends and Influence People*. My dad had recommended *Success Through a Positive Mental Attitude* by W. Clement Stone as well. It was a huge book for me. I just learned a lot about how persistence, an open attitude, and listening pays off long term; that's stuck with me through the years. It's also good to have a sense of humor.

That's an excellent book. Naturally, your dad inspired you as well along the way, but was there anyone else in particular that stood out?

Chris Webb: As far as my career goes, that first guy that I worked for in 1991 spurred me on. He was a very professional guy, the way he ran his operation. He treated everybody nicely. He developed the deep relationships with people they would bring in. So he's kind of a relationship guy who was consistent through the years. He wasn't necessarily an expert in all areas, but he would develop his relationships. He was a very prominent golfer in the Chicago land area too, so that gave him a relaxed setting where he could speak freely. He would always send letters to people after he met them; handwritten notes. He was also a real gentleman. He would surround himself with other professionals as well and not try to pretend that he knew everything. For example, a lot of times these companies don't have a relationship with the best providers but they are connected with people they bring in who do have the contracts and the respect of the carrier. So, he was just a great relationship builder and a real gentleman in the way he handled himself and expanded his business. I've tried to emulate that type of image. I've always heard and looked at him as a role model regarding the way I'd like to operate my business.

Yes, that's an excellent story. Thanks for sharing that. What drives you to get you out of bed every morning to help people? What's your passion? What's deep down?

Chris Webb: It's just helping people and educating them, so they are comfortable with areas that are sometimes tough. I tell you, one of the things that actually, I see more often than I like, I guess because of the business I'm in...Checking the business section of The *Chicago Tribune* every morning, at the back of the business section, are the obituaries. I scan them now, especially as I get older. I look through it briefly, but if I see a picture of a younger person, I'll tend to read the obit. I mean if it's somebody in their 50's or younger that's passed away, about 6 or 7 times out of 10, at the bottom of that obituary, it says, instead of flowers, send money to the Smith or whomever's Children's Education Fund. So in other words, the person did not buy any insurance that would have taken care of the family. The family wouldn't be needing to go out asking for distributions from friends and family who possibly don't even have money for their own kid's education and wellbeing let alone someone else's. So it just makes me sad. I see stories like that, or I run into business owners that don't have or have put off buying life insurance or disability insurance or long-term care insurance. There's just an enormous opportunity to help people. I just know that there're tons of people out there that need my help. And so that's what kind of gets me going every day. I enjoy meeting new people and hearing their story. I guess I've gotten to a point now, after being in the business for 25 years (and I cannot remember who said this next part so I'll paraphrase it) but his philosophy, and take on insurance (and I agree with it), is that it's about chemistry and timing. I make it my business in my business to go out and meet a bunch of people... if I meet somebody, and I feel like there's a good chemistry between us and I like the person, they like me, then I'll follow up with them. Now it might not be the right time for them to utilize my services, but I'll keep in touch. Everyone's life changes over time. Insurance is that "thing" when people need it, I will be there at that opportunity; when there's change going on out there. It creates opportunities. So that's the philosophy I've stuck with.

That's a good thing to live by. I mean you don't want to work with a bunch of people that you don't have chemistry with for sure.

Chris Webb: They're downers. You know I don't want to work with downers. I want to work with people that may have some challenges to solve, but if they have a positive attitude, I'm there.

What would you say or what would be the most natural obstacle preventing the reader from having the proper coverage or the appropriate insurance? You mention that by looking at the obituaries, you're finding that people don't even have the basics. So what kind of advice would you give?

Chris Webb: I think people just take for granted that everything works out without putting together a plan, or they've just been so busy that they haven't had time to focus on even the essentials. They're so busy with their kids and doing their work that it's just hard. Time is such a precious commodity these days that people just don't get a plan unless someone lays out the questions... What I've seen through the years is that people buy it when they are working on their checklist or are working on some other type of insurance related need, and it comes up. Otherwise, they put it up on a shelf, and they're like, phew, okay, yes, I do need to get to that and complete it. Sometimes, for example, someone gets married, and they buy a life policy, or they have a child. All of a sudden, they progress in their career, their income is five times what it was 7 or 8 years before when they bought the first policy, they buy a big house, they have three kids, and yet they still haven't readdressed their insurance needs. Their insurance needs have changed, but they just have not maybe had the energy to resurrect the conversation. It's not an exciting topic, kind of like estate planning, kind of like when somebody has to talk to the estate planner. It starts with someone else who dies or a disability comes into question; it's not a place where people want to go that often. I get it. I understand it. When it does happen, it's so crucial to have the right coverage for your business, for your home, for your family. I mean it makes a huge difference to a family and a business if they have the right coverage.

You are so right! In this fast paced economy this issue can get passed people. And of course, they think they can't afford it. So what would be some of the biggest misconceptions that they might be having about this?

Chris Webb: People think, oh my gosh, it's so expensive, it's so expensive. If somebody gets started early with insurance, and term insurance is a perfect example, you can qualify more easily, generally... For a couple of thousand dollars, $2,000 or $3,000 a year, you may be eligible for $5 million worth of term insurance. For a couple of hundred dollars a month, $250 a month, we just got $5 million worth of coverage for a young doctor. It would go a long way towards taking care of his family if something were to happen to him. It's just I think people believe it's a lot more expensive, or it's a lot more time-consuming to get examined and it's not the case. If somebody gets your information, we can get the info mapped out and get it done. I think it's just being willing to have the conversation and then realizing that it's not as time-consuming or expensive as the misinformation that might be out there. We can also insure risks at a higher level than we used to be able to offer as well.

What about some of the other challenges that people… I know I even started running through my mind. Is it like are these people perfectly healthy?

Chris Webb: As it relates to life insurance, there are some issues rarely regarded as disrupting the ability to get insured, such as speeding tickets, family history, etc., but we've seen it all from cancer to heart disease, diabetes, M.S., and in many cases we can find them insurance at some level. We have the advantage of being an independent agency and can tap on the best fit since we have many insurance carriers to access.

So yeah, that's good that you can provide that service to people.

Chris Webb: The thing is, being an independent agency, we don't use just the prominent companies you hear on the street. They have one bowl, and they've got one company. If their business can't help you, they're done. We love challenges. We thrive on trying to find the fit. That's how we add value to a situation where somebody's got a unique situation. In a lot of cases, we're able to solve those, not always, but we'll try. That's very satisfying and most of the time, it works out.

Absolutely. That's great. Can you tell us and describe how you've taken somebody with one of those cases and helped them out? You described a couple of them, but could you give us one more?

Chris Webb: I got referred to a gentleman who was an internist about 15 years ago. He had epilepsy, but it was controlled by the use of several medications. He bought some disability insurance, but he wanted to buy more disability insurance. His father-in-law, at that time, was an insurance agent, and his father-in-law said he absolutely would not be able to get more disability insurance. So I was talking to the guy and promised to make some calls. I made lots of calls and I found a company that, in fact, would write him for epilepsy because his epilepsy was under control. Now, what happened after that was the meds he was taking stopped working for his epilepsy. So he got to the point where he couldn't be with a patient because he would have seizures where he would blank out for a minute or two. He couldn't practice medicine anymore.

The insurance company paid. It was an additional $5,000 or $6,000 a month tax-free that this policy got him. He's on the website now, and I have an interview with him on my website. He still, to this day, when I talk to him, says, "You saved my life." You saved my life because you helped get me this policy. And then that extra $5,000 or $6,000 a month tax-free has made all the difference. He's still receiving his disability amount, for probably 12 years now. It's always a feel good for me. When I have a bad day, I think back about that triumph. Five people down the road may tell me to go pound sand, but I go back and think about that guy.

Oh definitely, that's a great story and thanks for sharing that. What would be your best piece of advice to someone who's considering purchasing coverage and having the right policy for whatever they're doing? What would be your best piece of advice to them?

Chris Webb: I'd say work with somebody that's independent. Work with someone that's local so that you can establish a long-term relationship with them, and the other thing I'd say as it relates to most insurance, raise the deductible. People I run into all the time have these low deductibles. Well, you know, my take on insurance, for the most part, is, particularly for home or your health insurance, have a higher deductible. In many cases, insurance is meant for catastrophic reasons, the fire that burnt down your house or the large health insurance claim. Also, try, with all things being equal, go with the better company. Look at the ratings of the carrier.

Great advice. Also great nuggets. If somebody's ready to get started with you, what's the best way to get a hold of you?

Chris Webb: Either by phone or email. I have a direct phone number, which is (847) 235-6001 and my email's chriswebb@webbfg.com.

Great. This concludes our interview. Thank you very much for your nuggets.

Chris Webb: Appreciate it. Thank you.

WEBSITE:
www.webbfg.com

EMAIL:
chriswebb@webbfg.com

FACEBOOK:
https://www.facebook.com/chris.webb

LINKEDIN:
https://www.linkedin.com/in/chriswebbinsurance

TWITTER
https://twitter.com/webbgolfer

PHONE

(847) 235-6001

Visionary Business Strategist

Filling the White Space Void

Keith was always a commissioned salesman and liked the ability to be financially responsible for his livelihood based on his own efforts. He enjoys working with people and has a knack for being able to make people feel comfortable, open up and share their challenges. Keith worked at three different radio stations and the last one forced him to face a simple truth: he wasn't comfortable playing corporate politics to get promoted.

Shortly after this realization, Keith set up a meeting with both the General Manager and his Local Sales Manager at the last station where he worked. He turned in his resignation; and then at the same time asked them to hire him as an independent contractor to handle all their value-add marketing programs. He was prepared with a full proposal, including his monthly fee plus commission based on his performance. The General Manager

63

signed the document on the spot. That's when Keith became an entrepreneur.

Years ago he saw Arthur Blank speak at an entrepreneur's conference. It was when Arthur was launching Home Depot in Atlanta, and he spoke of his vision for the company. At the time, there were only neighborhood hardware stores, and most national chains were very similar. Many at the conference asked: Who would need such a big hardware store? Who would shop there? They didn't see a need for it. But that's not what Arthur thought. He had a vision of what Home Depot could be and articulated it very clearly.

Keith remembers thinking: "This guy has a crystal ball. He can see the future, and this *is* going to happen". He saw Arthur's clarity, passion, commitment and willingness to go against the grain. Arthur Blank inspired Keith to believe in his vision and dreams. Just because a few people cannot immediately see what is possible doesn't mean it does not exist or that there is not a need for it.

It was a transforming experience.

Conversation with Keith Kriegler

All right Keith, thanks again for joining us. So let's get right into it. Tell me about your business and the types of clients that you help.

Keith Kriegler: Our company is White Space Marketing (www.whitespacemktg.com). The inspiration behind the name is that it's about all the new possibilities that can open up when you look at every aspect of a situation with fresh eyes and fresh thinking to find the key insights. In other words, "White Space" means "opportunities."

Every brand has them, whether they are emerging or stagnant; big or small; traditional or unconventional, companies all have opportunities to stand out and command consumer's attention. That's where our team shines: zeroing in and helping clients identify those insights that will lead to an opportunity ripe for growth; something their competitors have missed.

We like to say we are a new kind of brand advocacy agency, dedicated to changing "what is" to "what could, *and* should, be." We partner with active client collaborators who are just as dedicated to discovering new opportunities to grow their business. Together, we help them build emotional connections with their consumers and, ultimately, help them make more money. After all, that's what marketing is about.

So, that's the 'big picture' of our name and what we offer clients. Now, you asked about the types of clients White Space helps.

We work with mid-size and Fortune 1000 companies across a diverse range of industries — consumer packaged goods, technology, mobile, consumer products and services. Our work includes both business-to-consumer and business-to-business marketing as most all marketing entails working with a company's sales force and their internal teams, in addition to their distribution channels and retail partners.

Some companies we work with aren't typically viewed as 'traditional' marketers. Maybe they used to advertise, but have suspended that during a mature cycle. Or maybe their industry is new to the idea of brand-building entirely. These types of challenges give our team a chance to apply our unique approach to help re-energize their go-to-market strategy and generate revenue. In fact, we're currently working with a national real estate company and a health and wellness hand sanitizer brand to help them forge new ground and find *their* White Space.

Clients often tell us that they don't have the time, resources or skill sets in order to focus on identifying new opportunities for growth. They don't want to be a 'me too' brand, yet they are challenged with balancing their day-to-day work with focusing on their needs for future growth. They're very cognizant of the clutter that exists in the market yet find it hard to break away from their current tasks to think about how to find new, untapped ways to reach consumers and increase sales.

We understand these limitations. That's why we want our clients to think of us as an extension of their team. We offer the insights and talent needed to help them get things done and succeed. Often, we tell them we'll do the heavy lifting so they can stay focused on the big picture. Knowing that White Space will deliver targeted, strategic solutions and seamlessly execute marketing programs allows our clients to breathe a sigh of relief.

I've talked a bit about the 'what' and the 'who.' Let me wrap up this section with a bit about the 'how.'

White Space uses a combination of traditional research (focus groups, qualitative and quantitative studies) and experiential methods (field immersion) to gain key insights about our clients' categories, emerging trends and competitive landscapes. Gathering this type of intel is critical and can't be done sitting behind a desk and searching online.

In collaboration with our clients, we think about how and where consumers use a client's product or service. Then we conduct market visits and actually 'live' the consumer experience by going to the places where their brands are sold, similar brands are sold, and products used. This process, in addition to the insights gleaned from the traditional research, gives us the inspiration to help them identify *their* White Space.

*That is a huge problem with business owners working **in** the business instead of **on** the business. This leads us to the next question: What led you to this field and how did you get started in this business?*

Keith Kriegler: As an idea guy, I've always been very passionate about marketing and helping clients find new ways to evolve their brands to solve consumers' continually changing needs.

I spent time working at several agencies in Chicago, including being a partner in an integrated marketing agency for over 12 years. In my 20+ years in sales and marketing, I've had the opportunity to strategize and execute most types of marketing including digital strategy, social media, shopper marketing, experiential, consumer and trade promotions, to name a few. And, I have been fortunate to work with many leading brands such as Allstate, Hewlett-Packard, Nabisco, Maytag, UPS, and Verizon.

After years of spending time with clients at a variety of companies, I kept seeing how challenged senior marketers are to be able to think beyond what they're doing today in order to focus on how they can expand their business tomorrow. The other factor is how competitive the landscape is across many disciplines: brick and mortar, online presence, emerging media, pop-up stores, experiential activities, etc.

Seeing how limited clients are with both time and resources, I realized the growing need to support their efforts to be innovative thinkers. The desire to think beyond the obvious and find new ways to bring their brand to market – either via new channels of distribution, brand extensions, synchronizing their online and offline marketing, or forming mutually beneficial cross-promotional partnerships - it's about making their brand the hero in solving consumers' needs. Often times consumers don't realize they have the need until they see the product and have that 'ah ha' moment. That's when we know we've succeeded in finding *their* White Space.

With all my experience of developing targeted strategies, providing exceptional client service and being respectful of clients' time, I understand what it takes to build a team with the know-how to exceed client expectations time and time again. I wanted to take that knowledge and create something special. These qualities are something client partners, who are eager to make a difference, would rally around.

My goal was to establish a firm where mining for the opportunity was the central focus. Then, early last year, I met with a former client who is a highly respected, knowledgeable researcher. She was going through a job transition at the time, and having been on the client side at many leading companies including McDonald's, General Mills and Alberto Culver, she validated the need clients have to be visionary about their business, and the challenges they face in having the time and resources to do so.

It was then that White Space became a reality and together we began working on the positioning for the agency.

You know, I've interviewed a lot of entrepreneurs and business owners and I love asking this question: Was there a book or a person that inspired you along the way?

Keith Kriegler: The first person that comes to mind is Howard Schultz, Starbucks founder. His first book, *"Pour Your Heart Into It"*, really resonated with me. I often read business books because I'm very inspired by entrepreneurs, but he is a phenomenal example of identifying opportunities, gaining internal alignment, and building a culture of community. I read about how he had to close down one of his first stores here in Chicago because of location and weather issues, but persevered with his concept and made it what it is today.

I appreciate how he saw cafés in Italy bringing people together over coffee, and giving them a place to congregate in a warm, comfortable environment. Bringing the idea to the states, and branding Starbucks as 'the third destination' to give people a place to get a reprieve from their day, is highly admirable. I believe seeing that opportunity, having the vision to bring it to life and overcoming many obstacles to bring the concept to fruition is a testament to his brilliance.

Of course there were many critics who said: "Nobody is going to pay three dollars for a cup of coffee. And, who has the time to go in and get it?" At the time it was mainly fast food restaurants and quick serve establishments where consumers went to get their coffee. No one at the time was offering the "consumer experience."

Schultz had this passion for using coffee to bring people together and saw the idea behind including comfortable furniture in Starbucks. He created a 'fifteen-minute escape' as he refers to it and he's continued to evolve the brand; that is highly admirable. This evolution of the brand includes taking care of the coffee growers and his staff (by offering health benefits for example). Now they're evolving with a whole new concept to continually grow Starbucks. I recently saw the VP of Marketing for Starbucks speak. He shared the company's commitment to continually evolving to meet consumer's needs; engaging the coffee growers; and, making their internal teams and store staff a part of the whole process to become one community. Their belief is that this type of community will be a benefit to the greater good of the world. That kind of commitment is very inspiring to me.

They take information from everybody at the company; yes, it's one person's vision, but it's how that vision is internalized, realized and executed that makes Starbucks such a huge success. It's such a collaborative process done with a lot of integrity — and a lot of trust and respect for the team. I truly admire that, and it's what I want for our company as we grow White Space.

You mentioned earlier in a previous comment about passion. What is it that really drives you to help the people that you help, and the companies?

Keith Kriegler: I thrive on helping clients see things in a different light, and giving them the assurance to know that we can accomplish great things together. Ideas they may not have thought of, or believed could be achieved.

Quick story: We were working with a mid-west regional office of Nabisco about ten years ago. At the time, they were the category leader in cookies and snack crackers and their goal was to leverage the equity of Oreo to grow their portfolio of cookies and snack crackers. This was going on at the time the term 'retailtainment' was very prominent in marketing. 'Retailtainment' referred to giving people a unique, memorable in-store experience. This was something that grocery chains were pressuring consumer packaged goods marketers to offer to help each chain create a competitive point of difference.

The program involved having children ages twelve and younger stack as many Oreo cookies as they could in thirty-seconds. The stacking event took place primarily in the front lobby of retail stores and was positioned against a duel end-cap display, in most instances. Nabisco provided retailers with the program based on their incremental purchases of Nabisco cookies and snack crackers.

It was a tiered, multi-level program with a designated number of winners per participating chain. Then a final 'stack off' was held at Riverfront Stadium leveraging Nabisco's sponsorship of the Cincinnati Reds. Our client believed so strongly in the program, that together, we went to Nabisco corporate to get incremental funding to execute.

The folks at Nabisco headquarters asked: "Are you sure we can do this? Do you really think that Kroger and Safeway will buy into it?" My response was: "Absolutely we can do this! Let's get a meeting with them and show them what the Oreo Stacking Contest can do for their stores. They're all about creating a retail experience for their customers, and you're Nabisco—the category leader! Let's leverage these iconic brands and show them what 'retailtainment' is all about."

And, we did. Year one, the program ran in 250 stores and Nabisco's sales increased by 79%. It was fantastic. I got a call from the senior vice president of marketing and he was blown away by the fact that we got two hundred and fifty stores to participate; the execution went flawlessly. Many of the chains called us shortly after the program ended and said: "We want to participate in next year's event." That had never happened in the history of the company. The program expanded to upwards of over 1,500 stores and then went national.

We achieved similar success working with UPS on the launch of The UPS Stores. Their goal was to generate revenue on non-shipping services. The key insight we learned from research is the UPS brand equity lies in their brown trucks and uniforms. Everyone knows that they ship packages, but our challenge was to inform consumers about all the other services UPS offers and to incent them to use those services.

The program we created was called "UPS Delivers" and entailed an experiential program involving hiring actors, who served as the UPS 'drill team'. The actors drove around UPS stores in brown uniforms (yes, we got permission to use the vehicles and uniforms). They would drive the truck around the radius of stores during morning and evening rush hours. The actors would stop the truck, jump out and (in flash mob style) stop consumers in the street and rhythmically chant UPS Delivers "packages, mailboxes, printing, business services and so much more".

To drive store traffic, we partnered with a nearby Starbucks and handed consumers a flyer with a coffee cup holder. When people brought the cup holder into The UPS Store and got it stamped 'UPS Delivers', they received a free cup of coffee compliments of UPS and it gave us the two to three minutes we needed to inform them about all of UPS' services. It was exciting, unconventional and highly effective.

The program drove great awareness and visibility for The UPS Store services, resulting in strong sales increases on non-shipping services. The program was so successful that it ran for several years in over 15 markets.

These examples show how we make things possible when they seem impossible. Once we help a client achieve success, it gives them the confidence to take on their next challenge, and savor another victory, and another.

The most difficult part of the process in any situation is earning a client's trust. My team and I are committed to helping our clients be successful. We don't quit until they feel a sense of accomplishment. That's what drives me. That's what drives the entire team at White Space. When our clients feel that they've been victorious and say, 'wow, we did it!' then we all feel a great sense of pride.

That's great. What would be some common obstacles preventing the reader from establishing their brand?

Keith Kriegler: We already talked about the lack of time and resources that prevents clients from taking on new challenges; they're too busy day-to-day. They are entrenched in just getting their work done. It's hard for them to say, "Okay, let's take a step back and focus on three to six months from now, or a year from now and start to break new ground. Let's start to find out where the opportunities are, and understand the market trends?" We are focused on moving our clients' brands forward so we can grow their businesses, and get ahead of the curve so they are not another copycat brand.

The other part is gaining internal alignment among the stakeholders. In fact, last week we had a kick off meeting and it was supposed to be with five stakeholders. One was too busy and wasn't able to attend the meeting and another person said, "I'll do what everybody else wants to do." The client agreed to move forward with the project, because they felt a sense of urgency and couldn't afford *not* to move forward. If they did, it would have delayed their planning process, and would have affected their whole team's ability to hit their revenue goals and potential bonuses for the year. This type of behavior is common in many organizations.

Sometimes, depending upon the company, there is one primary stakeholder who rallies the team and says "We're going to make this happen. I need your support. Who's in?" Those are true pioneers within the organization, and they are great! They are usually the people who are seen as the leaders within the company, regardless of their titles. That's because they're committed to owning their businesses and bringing new ideas to the table to move the needle.

Another obstacle is that while people are supposed to be in the field surveying their stores and the competition, often times they don't have the time to do so. This hinders their thinking about what's really taking place in the market and how the competition is eroding their market share.

As part of our due diligence to them, our team discusses where they feel the competition is gaining traction on them, and where they are challenged in growing their businesses in their current distribution model – whether it's brick and mortar stores or online. Our team digs deep into a variety of areas to understand what's taking place in the market. We document it through videos, pictures, social media audits, and then develop an executive summary of what we found in the places we visited.

Our point of difference is that we tell them what's taking place, what the implications are to their businesses, and most importantly, what they can do about it.

Can you share another story about how you've actually helped someone to get from point A to point B?

Keith Kriegler: We're helping a client grow their business by using alternate channels to educate end-users on the value of having a recognized brand name of hand sanitizer in their offices, and how that helps them build their reputation.

We're conducting man-on-the-street interviews to learn consumers' perspectives about having recognizable brands in medical professional offices – dentists, doctors, minute clinics, etc. Due to the importance of cleanliness today to prevent germs from spreading and heightened awareness about sanitization, using a known brand gives consumers' confidence that their dentist is not cutting corners, and genuinely cares about their well-being. Having a trusted brand in their offices helps these medical professionals build their reputations and win consumer confidence.

We're creating this story using the video content that will live on microsites, and highlight key points about the benefits the brand offers. There's a lead generation campaign that drives these practitioners, and their influencers (hygienists, office managers) to the microsites to learn more information about the product's benefits and to register to get a free trial.

In addition to living on the microsites, the video content is being used in many ways to support the distributors, get the message to the end-users at professional conferences and to support their sales staff. We're making it fun and engaging. Our goal is to have the practitioner's say: "I never thought of that but it makes a lot of sense. I use the brand at home and can see how patients would want to see the brand they know and trust in the office, not some generic brand."

So far, the results have been terrific. It's an innovative approach to helping the client fill *their* White Space, and it's been very well received. We're in the early stages of the program, but conversions have increased, sales are growing and it's getting a lot of buzz within the company. The client is thrilled that he brought this 'game-changing' idea (his term) to help the company expand its business.

Got it. Moving forward, what would be the first thing the reader should do when they're ready to enter a new market, or establish their brand in a marketplace?

Keith Kriegler: Call us! We welcome the opportunity to talk with them about their challenges and needs. We would start with a collaborative discussion with stakeholders to learn their answers to the following types questions:

- What is it that you are trying to accomplish?
- What's preventing you from achieving your goals?
- Who in your category is doing a great job, and what is it they're doing that makes it so great?
- What are your channels of distribution and who oversees these channels?
- How do you define success?

Once we have a solid understanding of their business and answers to these questions, then we want to dive into understanding the competitive landscape, what the emerging trends are, and what their research shows about their category.

Based on this information, we would then make a recommendation to conduct experiential methods to visit the places where consumers buy their products/services and 'like' brands to see firsthand what the consumer experience is about. Doing this provides us with great insight about where new opportunities exist for them.

Once all that information is collected, a strategic plan is developed that serves as a roadmap for them to be able to develop a long-term plan to grow their business. We'll prioritize the ideas based on their ability to execute and generate revenue growth. Some ideas are short-term and enable them to capitalize on the low-hanging fruit versus long-term opportunities that may take more planning.

Then we meet with all the stakeholders to show them the plan, gain their buy-in, vet it out and develop roles in how we can support them in the execution phase. This enables us to become an extension of their team; providing them with the resources, time and skill sets needed to bring the concepts to life so they can *own their* **White Space**.

The readers are ready to find out more about you and how you can help them, what's the best way for them to do that?

WEBSITE:
www.SH.whitespacemktg.com

EMAIL:
keith@whitespacemktg.com
info@whitespacemktg.com

LINKEDIN:
https://www.linkedin.com/in/keithkriegler

SKYPE:
Keithkriegler

PHONE:
Cell: (312) 415-5297
Office: (312) 281-1470

Result Driver

Helping You Get Focused on the Results That Matter

Rachel's personal mission is to drive Results That Matter. She believes so wholeheartedly in this purpose that she had it engraved into a locket ring she wears every day to help maintain focus and decision-making abilities.

She wants every situation and encounter in her life to be better off for having been present. A bad mood carries over to everyone else - and good energy carries further, and with lasting results. She strives to be that propulsion that makes great things happen. If it is nothing more than giving a TSA clerk an extra smile on a long day, Rachel cares if she is creating a positive ripple effect.

Her husband, Mark, children and extended family are incredibly important to her. As she says, "More important than her next breath." Because of them, she can pursue her dreams. Not everyone has this foundation and she realizes all the time how nothing at all would be possible without the support of her family.

Professionally, Rachel uses her result-oriented perspective to drive purposeful, game-changing meetings and events for her clients. Rachel helps organizations first see the competitive advantage of strategic events, then helps them get out of their own way. Her company Advanced Events, Inc. ensures that clients always gain and never lose with each of their face-to-face interactions. Who knew success can be found by holding clients accountable to their own growth strategy!

When priorities clash and everything is important, keeping focus isn't so easy! Organizations are often left wondering about the ROI on their largest marketing efforts. She solved this problem by developing a diagnostic tool (called "Alignment Advantage") used up front to align and clarify stakeholders with the desired outcome. She and her team talk results first and foremost.

Everyone defines success differently. Whether success means revenue growth, knowledge transfer or increased engagement, Advanced Events starts by diving deep and asking the tough questions. They continually challenge assumptions and look for the right approach that supports the specific objective. Rachel makes sure they have a complete understanding of what assumptions, barriers, behaviors or other business agendas influence success.

Conversation with Rachel Nielsen

Rachel, thanks again for being a part of this project, Success Hackers. We'll just get started right from the box. Tell us about the business and the types of customers you help.

Rachel Nielsen: Basically, we help organizations grow business using face-to-face engagements as a strategic competitive advantage. Success can be defined in many different ways. Whatever that success or growth is that they're looking for, we help them clarify and unify as to how they will achieve those results that matter to their business.

We know that face-to-face engagements are the most powerful way to influence an audience and control a message. Whether that's a meeting with two people or an event with 2,000, or a conference of 15,000, being able to control your message and influence your audience for a very specific targeted outcome is really powerful.

A lot of our work is through aligning visionaries on what it is specifically that they want to accomplish. Sometimes owners are so close to the details that they need help to define and simplify what it is they are trying to achieve. It's amazing how many times we encounter different interpretations of what success looks like.

Awesome. Not only corporate folks, but you're also helping business owners and entrepreneurs on a smaller scale, as well.

Rachel Nielsen: Exactly. Our favorite audience isn't one particular vertical. Our ideal partner is the business owner or CEO, who understands that bringing people together is a vital part of their growth strategy.

Do you find that the advent of the internet, and online learning, and things like that, that it's still the key to being face-to-face, obviously?

Rachel Nielsen: Absolutely. Like I said, the only way that you can control your message delivery is when it is live. What I mean is that if you want to refine the message midway through, it can only happen when you are receiving live feedback. A video is an excellent way to convey a message, but you can't react, you can't refine it mid-process, ultimately you can't CONTROL the message.

Excellent point. With video being so popular for initial exposure it's always good to take it offline. What led you to this field and how did you get started in this business?

Rachel Nielsen: Originally, I was in the Chicago sports scene, working at both Comiskey Park, when it first opened in the new stadium, and then as part of the opening management team at the United Center. Seeing how people were coming together in that live environment was infectious. I was enamored observing how people interacted in groups. The 1996 Democratic National Convention as a prime example.

It wasn't until years later that I realized the untapped POWER in groups of people gathering. This was when I was working with a major international corporation during a re-branding effort, where the CEO wanted to transform decades of stagnate corporate behavior and shift flat-lined public opinion of the products.

It was just so transparent to me that, to stay relevant and competitive in a marketplace, you had to impact people in a particular manner. We were part of something so incredibly significant in changing how 1,200 people did business for 30

83

years. In one afternoon we literally changed how they went back to the office and did business.

It was just crazy how I saw lives transformed because of the way we methodically designed an event experience with a systematic delivery of a particular message. We changed business at that very moment.

You go deeper than the logistics part of an event. You mold the message. Is that what I understand?

Rachel Nielsen: The message is one component. We have a two-fold approach. Logistics are always going to be important because you have to do what you say you're going to do. You have to deliver – that's a given.

Where we excel, our sweet spot, is the period before that message is defined. Here is the secret...the moment of why an event is conceptualized is the essence and truest representation of the business result that is intended to be driven by holding the event. From that moment on, the result (real objective) is challenged by outside influences. We help unearth the expected results of the event, and then deliver on those pure strategic intentions.

Let me explain it a bit further...we call this the Alignment Advantage. The Alignment Advantage is a diagnostic process of getting key stakeholders on the same page, saying the same thing.

Let me give you a quick analogy. Somebody could say, "We're going to have a reception for our board." It's pretty straight forward. You want to have an appreciation dinner for the board before the annual meeting.

Reception can be defined in probably 100 different ways. Is it up on a rooftop and you're enjoying the scenery?

Or, is it in a board room because you want to convey an intimate and critical message to only a few people?

Do you wish to have an up-close, intimate conversation, or do you want have spouses there in order to bond relationships?

The way that you go about it is entirely different, depending on the particular outcome that you want to achieve.

Through our Alignment Advantage process, key stakeholders are required to have the complete conversation. We pose tough questions many people are not prepared to answer. Often the response involves legacy getting in the way of progress. How many times do we hear...We've always done it this way? Why wouldn't we do it this way again?"

Asking pointed questions and forcing the conversation is never easy. And it really isn't easy when we need to point out, if they are sabotaging themselves when legacy habit decisions interfere with strategic thought.

Famous last words: we've always done it this way. Those are the most famous words in the world, I think.

Rachel Nielsen: Yes. I'm not a fan. I often think to myself? If we were starting from the onset of civilization, would we do it the same way again? I don't think we would.

That's an excellent point. Every entrepreneur that I've spoken with, or businessperson, has been influenced by a book. Do you recall any particular book that's influenced you along the way?

Rachel Nielsen: I've been influenced by people, more than a book. Books are fantastic, and the written word is incredibly powerful. Yet I would say that people in my life have influenced me much more significantly than an author I've only read. Ironically, many of the people I am thinking of have written books too.

Anybody in particular stand out?

Rachel Nielsen: So many. One of the earliest in my professional career was from a colleague at the United Center who told me to "act as if I am in the position that I wanted, not the one I was in."

That's a good nugget, right there.

Rachel Nielsen: It was. It was very, very powerful. Another person telling me not to be afraid to be surrounded by intelligent people gave me the confidence to try anything, and to never be afraid to ask a question.

Another good one.

Rachel Nielsen: The list of those who have impacted me goes on and on. Sharing meaningful experiences and conversations with people are what inspires me.

I always liked the saying that if you're the smartest person in the room, you're in the wrong place.

Rachel Nielsen: I often find myself enamored by the people who I share my time, personally and professionally. I'm like, what am I doing running with such great and interesting people? I just don't know how I deserve all that.

You mentioned a little bit earlier about some passion that you had, but what really drives you deep down to help the people that you help?

Rachel Nielsen: It's how I live my life. I even wear this in my Takohl Treasure Ring. My motto is "Results Matters". It is the result of my actions that I use to judge my own worth. I found a way in business to impact organizations. For nonprofit organizations, we're impacting entire industries. For the corporate clients, we're propelling their mission too.

In my personal life, it's the same thing. It's the result that I'm driving. I'm not worried about being right, (although my husband might argue otherwise.)Really, I'm not worried about being right. I am concerned about what momentum are we creating? What is the impact? What is the result that lasts long after I was here? I don't care if it is checking out at the grocery line. If I'm in a bad mood, and I'm snippy to the clerk, the result that I have left there is not what I want to perpetuate. I want to be recognized for positive impact, not negative. Like I said, results matter to me.

What's the biggest misconception people have when they come to you about pulling off a successful event?

Rachel Nielsen: I suppose misconception and bad habit are similar. For us it is really difficult when conversations start by talking about what can't be done versus what can be done. Here is an example...Let's take a scenario where a motivational speaker is needed. Let's say Patrick Lencioni is mentioned to play this role of motivational speaker. He is a highly sought-after, amazing author. He's a very powerful presenter, an incredibly humble person with reach beyond his means, into hearts, into souls, into lives of every level of an organization. If someone's talking about, "We can't afford him," or, "He's out of our reach," we're already limiting ourselves.

I would rather talk about what can be done. How can we approach it that it is possible, and can still generate the same result, the same impact, without necessarily the limitations that we're originally putting upon ourselves? (Example, invite him for back to back sessions, and open the latter to a wider audience with paid entrance fees that cover the original budget shortfall.)

Can you talk about an individual, or a company, or someone that you've helped overcome some of these obstacles of successfully pulling off an event?

Rachel Nielsen: Sure. Give me a parameter. We have so many.

Let's say that someone had a mindset of, just like you described. Maybe you've got this big vision of having this event, and their mentality is, I'd like to do this, but I can't afford it. How could they pull off an event that they could afford and have the same impact?

Rachel Nielsen: I'm going to go a little bit larger, but it certainly comes out of the budget limitation. Our client was an organization in the financial sector. I'm sure you'll remember back in 2008 and 2009; this industry was getting hit hard all over the media, all over the world. This organization was in jeopardy, because so many of the members, literally their industries, were being eaten up in a matter of weeks. They were either being merged, they were being acquired, or they were simply going out of business at a rapid, rapid pace. Our client was in a situation to determine how did they, as an organization, survive, and continue to serve the sector?

What we did was started analyzing, what is the real value that this organization could provide remaining members? Forget about just the membership dues and trying to renew them. What is the real value that organization is offering to its members, and which audience in specific?

They knew that the audience that made the decision to, one, stay in business, and, two, remain a member of this organization, was the CEOs. The next step was to determine how to provide such an incredible amount of value to them that the membership dues are the one thing that survives budget cuts?

We ended up creating a new conference to gather only CEOs. By the way, they had to pay to come and attend this meeting. The gold they needed...facilitated problem-solving, solution-oriented think tanks. There were plenty of caveats; a safe environment had to be created for open sharing despite competitors in the same room. Focusing messaging and value around the need for collaboration in the industry is what helped propel the sector through this terrible time.

Interesting

Rachel Nielsen: Very, counter-intuitive. You are creating opportunities to spend more money. Keep in mind, this was with a zero start budget, so everything had to be self-funded by those who were attending. This summit had not been done before, so history was not available to rely on as a success indicator. We had to focus entirely on delivering a very intimate experience, over a short time frame, with deep impact, for high ranking individuals.

That's a great example. Thank you for sharing that.

Rachel Nielsen: You're welcome. Thank you for helping me dive into it.

What would be the first thing that the reader should do if they're ready to have an event, or they're thinking about doing some large conference? What would be the first thing that you would tell them?

Rachel Nielsen: Have they defined the results that matters? Do they know what impact they need to exist long after the event?

Could you go a little bit deeper in that?

Rachel Nielsen: Sure. Somebody who was saying, "Let's have a conference. Let's do this. Let's gather people." In that initial spark of a conversation, that is where the real value lives. There is a reason during that thought process or that conversation that says, "You know what? My business, my life, will be better off if I have this type of conference."

That moment is when they're identifying the ideal audience and the value that needs to be delivered, along with the specific benefit to be derived from hosting a conference.

Everything from that point forward is confusing. The real moment of pure "this is what we need to drive" is in that initial spark.

What is that particular result that matters? It might be a relationship that needs to be expanded. It might be a conversation that's difficult to initiate across new verticals. It might be that, let's be real selfish. Let's say they're going to make a significant amount of money by selling this opportunity. It doesn't matter what that result is; we want to gain clarity in to that result they are trying to drive. The beauty of what Advanced Events does is help our clients get out of their own way and hold on to that essence.

Excellent. Then, let's lead to the most important thing they should think about right out of the box. I know that you just mentioned what's the end result, but what would be something immediately following that?

Rachel Nielsen: How committed are they to getting that particular result?

I don't mean from a financial or a resource perspective. I mean that people say they want to change, or be different, or new, or better, or more. Then, when resistance is met, opinions change.

It's really about the level of commitment.

I'll give you a mundane example with two different extremes. One extreme will be with the CEO Think Tank Summit that I talked about in the earlier example. The organization commits to creating the exclusive CEO only, safe environment for a collaborative solution-oriented think-tank. There could be a lot of people who want in, and maybe they don't all fit the CEO profile. What happens when a call from a highly involved vendor partner is received claiming, "I'm your supporter, and I want to come, too."

A robust conversation may be necessary to explain to the supplier with deep pockets but who doesn't meet the attendee profile to say, "I'm sorry, you're not a CEO member. You're a vendor. This isn't the conference for you." That's a tough conversation to have, and many of the best cave when big money is on the line.

If that individual were let in, the safe environment would be challenged, and the entire conference is at risk.

If you're going to stay pure to what you want to deliver, you have to be prepared for difficult decisions along the way.

Or, another example is the tried and true "We're going to shake this up" request. Every entity is asking to shake things up. They want to do it differently. Not just different to be different, but purposefully different, relevant. Then they start letting legacy direct decisions.

"The Board says we have to have the reception the night before."

"Okay, but what you're trying to do is a one-day conference. Why would you do a reception the night before? You've explicitly put out a directive you're going to have an eight-hour day out of their office. You're now asking for an overnight accommodation."

"The Board says we have to do it."

The Board is going against what they said you wanted. See, through no direct fault of their own, they are no longer dedicated to the initial Result That Mattered beyond the Event.

It is very easy to be unknowingly off target.

Do you find that events are more successful during the week versus the weekend? What's your take on that?

Rachel Nielsen: There's a thought process behind scheduling events. The reality is, everyone has competition for their time. We focus much more on what the audience is receiving. The way we determine it is, what is the value beyond the event for this audience?

Here's one of my favorite analogies: if you're going to have an event, shift the perspective to the audience member, and determine why would that person choose to attend. For example, what is unique enough for this busy attendee to find compelling enough to attend? Why should this attendee base take time away from what they hold important to come to this particular event over another?

It's not so much the day of the week; it's really what is the attendee getting that drives if he or she is even willing to consider checking the calendar to attend?

So we analyze, who the attendee interacts with at the event. And we look at the structure in how time is spent. We help our clients find compelling reasons to those aspects before selecting a date on the calendar.

Have you found a sweet spot, as far as entrepreneurs that are offering events, or is each one of them different? A lot of people say, "You throw in bonuses that are more valuable than the actual price of admission, or it's a free event, and then relying on bonuses to fill the seats." Could you go into that a little bit?

Rachel Nielsen: There is a numerous amount of strategies that are employed to market and message what the experience is going to be. We use adult learning principles to impact thought processes more than anything else. It isn't just a proven strategy, one way or another.

Nothing that we do is one-size-fits-all. Everything is very bespoke and created individually for, again, creating that result that matters beyond the event. There are formulas and trends that we incorporate, but there is not a one-size-fits-all solution.

When you say "benefits beyond the conference," what would be some of those benefits, either coaching calls, or one-on-one coaching, or something like that? Is that what you're referring to, or something different?

Rachel Nielsen: I'll give you an example of a purpose beyond the event. Sponsors and strategic partnerships are heavy in every organization; this component is incorporated in to almost everything we encounter - corporate events, entrepreneurial startup company events, and in nonprofit industry organizations.

Key vendor/partner/supplier/ relationships need to drive value for these firms far beyond seeing their logo at an event.

We tend to lean towards creating sponsor packages that have a focus on what lives beyond the event for the sponsor company. We seek to understand what makes that company tick, so they can be positioned correctly to connect with the right people. It might be helping them cultivate a very specific audience for a workshop that they are presenting. It's, again, not only what's driving our direct client's value and their business success, but how are all the other people, the tentacles, of the organizations that they are also touching driving success. What is their value and how is this particular event benefiting those organizations beyond the direct event?

Got it. I've been told about companies that are taking money out of general marketing budgets and putting them into *sponsorship buckets. There's $52 billion just in the United States laying out there for sponsorships. Do you find that's the case?*

Rachel Nielsen: Certainly a growing trend. Even some of the startup corporations that we partner with are buying sponsorship packages. Again, we approach things from a result-oriented position, not so much just a front-end.

For example, I was talking with a strategic partner for a conference that just operated. They didn't feel that they received the return on their sponsorship they anticipated.

This company had gone to our client complaining. Here I am, invited to the conversation late in the game, and I inquired, "Besides the physical elements of the sponsorship package, what were the results that you were looking to accomplish when buying the sponsorship package?"

The company representative did not have a definite answer, just knew it "wasn't what we expected."

It is critical to know beforehand what you are looking to drive – impressions, relationships, contacts, proposals, hot leads, etc. If a company is specifically looking at building reputation and recognition, we would seek a far different sponsorship package than something geared toward making direct connections and networking with people.

Yes, there is a plethora of corporate money earmarked in budgets as a certain percentage toward sponsorships. Can you hear the voice, "Of the 28% marketing budget allocated in the fiscal operating fund, 14% will be funneled in to sponsorships, and the remaining 14% is going to be line itemed for direct advertising?"

Yes, there is somebody sitting back in an office making formula driven decisions. Then, the mistake we see, is there are very few people executing and paying attention to the particular opportunity and direct value of the sponsorships purchased.

Interesting. If somebody is ready to get started with you, or find out more about how you can help them, where do they go and what do you suggest they do?

Rachel Nielsen: There's our company website AdvancedEvents.net or, the one that starts you thinking from the very beginning is BeyondYourEvent.com

Organizations who are already thinking about what exists Beyond the Event are on the fast track for success.

For anyone seeking clarity on their organization's true objectives, the Alignment Advantage Consulting and Diagnostic are a standalone service that offers enormous immediate value.

Very good If somebody wants to get a hold of you immediately, how would they do that?

Rachel Nielsen: My direct line is (708)-528-0600. We also have a team number (708)-970-8000. My direct email is Rachel, R-A-C-H-E-L @advancedevents.net.

Awesome Rachel. That concludes our interview. You did a great job. Thank you!

WEBSITE:
www.advancedevents.net
www.BeyondYourEvent.com

SKYPE:
rachelynielsen

EMAIL:
rachel@advancedevents.net

LINKEDIN:
https://www.linkedin.com/in/rachelyoungnielsen

PHONE:
(708) 528-0600
(708)-970-8000

Leadership and Communications Expert

To Bring Out What is Awesome In You

John tried several things as a youngster. He did odd jobs for attorneys, worked at a gas station and even did a stint as a janitor with a custom made vacuum backpack. At the same time, he watched his Father work in corporate America and then saw him get a royal screwing for having integrity as an attorney. It wasn't lost on young John how much happier his father was once he went out on his own. Since then John was never really interested in a "job." He also sang in a band when he was young, and that was a lot of fun for him yet he never really thought about how entrepreneurial it was, until now.

John remembers watching a speaker at TEDxSantaMonica at the same time he was considering starting his current business. The speaker on stage was smart; he had all the hard skills (which John admitted to me that he always felt he didn't have and which made him feel like he was somehow "less than"). The speaker had a very compelling message. However, it was so awkward and painful to watch him up on stage that it completely ruined his message and obscured his great ideas and offerings. At that moment, John realized that if he just got over himself; if he just dropped the chip on his shoulder about hard skills and soft skills, he could make a real difference for someone like that. And that was the moment this thing became real for him. His life's path finally made sense.

Conversation with John Bates

Thanks again for joining us today for the Success Hackers book project. So tell us a little bit about your business and what types of customers that you're helping.

John Bates: Well, Tracy, my WHY - in the style of Simon Sinek - is to bring out what's awesome inside every person so it can live in the world and make a real difference! And what I *do* is leadership communication training. For my whole life, I've had what people call the soft skills. And, I always felt somehow that I was less than, or not as good as people who had the hard skills. You know, the scientist, the engineers, and the people who had a business degree, whatever it is. And what I saw a while ago, at one of the original TEDxSantaMonica events which was happening right when TEDx was a brand new phenomenon, and there was this guy up onstage speaking about a really interesting subject. He had all the hard skills. He was a former venture capitalist. He was doing something very interesting. And his speech wasn't really horrible, but what made it so awful for me was that it could've been very good and yet it was just awkward. I thought, if I just get over myself, I could actually make a difference for people like him. And so I put together a training, originally for TEDx speakers, and I based everything I did in (should be on) human evolutionary biology and human neurophysiology because I knew I was going to be talking to a lot of scientists and a lot of very logical people and I would have to show them not only *what* to do when it comes to great leadership communication, but *why* it would work. And what turned out to be great for me is that *everybody* actually likes to know not only *what* to do but *why* it works; not just scientists. I started with TED and TEDx events, doing a lot of training for TED and TEDx speakers, and then very quickly got asked to come into their companies and do my training for their top executives, sales teams, and presenters. Now, the bulk of my income and work is with companies like NASA, Boeing, IBM, Johnson & Johnson and Accenture where I work with their C-level and high-level executives, training them in how to be more effective leaders and communicators with a focus on, and basis in, human evolutionary biology and human neurophysiology.

Those are the people that you actually assist. So, you're going to these corporations and these people are successful in their own right already, but they're missing an element of communication when they're in front of somebody, right? Is that the way I understand it? And they're using the TED Talk's format to get their information out there.

John Bates: Yes, the TED *format* has become really popular as people see how effective it is to focus what you're saying, make it interesting, make it connected and make it short. A lot of the corporations I work with are doing things like internal TEDx-style talks when they want to do their all hands meeting. They want to get up in front of the team and give a TED-style talk. Many are even creating both internal and external videos of these talks to fire up the troops or explain their unique point of view in the market. So that's become quite a buzzword for people and I think what it really is shorthand for is: very effective, well thought-out, well-crafted and connected communication. And it's not just about being onstage. Certainly I train people to be onstage and to give effective presentations, but it's not just from the big stage. It's being onstage in air quotes, being in front of the board members, being in front of the all hands meeting, talking to just a few team members about an important project. It even makes a difference in one-on-one communication. I train people in the most important, key principles in communication and they work everywhere from one-on-one all the way up to one-to-millions, if that's what they're doing. And those principles have people be more effective communicators, which I believe is at the heart of being a truly effective leader.

Interesting. I'm glad you clarified that because I got my start inside corporate America speaking to all hands and things like that, from a corporate level. I like how you provide that to them as well. And what led you to this field and how did you get started?

John Bates: I grew up in Salt Lake City, Utah and I grew up Mormon. I got to do a couple of little speaking things in church. So I, like Aretha Franklin, started my career in church, but it wasn't quite the same. Then, what happened is that I've made all these really brilliant decisions by accident in my life, and one of those brilliant decisions I made by accident was to follow Joanie Babulos, who was the most beautiful girl in junior high school, into the Forensics class in high school. So when I was a freshman in high school, my best friend Jeff and I took Forensics because Joanie Babulos was taking Forensics. And that ended up being very lucky because our coach was ranked as one of the top 2 or 3 coaches in debate and Forensics anywhere in the world, and he was at my public high school, and I loved that guy. So, let me tell you a quick story about that, and please hang in there with me to the end. In high school, I won pretty much every contest I ever entered. I took first, second or third all the time. However, there was one time that I didn't and that judge actually found me 2 years later and apologized to me and told me that he had been regretting it ever since. He said I should've won that contest and he apologized. And here's the interesting thing about that. Yes, I did well, but it was *not* because I was special. I did only one thing different than anyone else: I had a world-class coach and that's the one thing I did, I was *coachable*. Being coachable is what had me win all those contests because I had a brilliant coach and I just did whatever he said. And so I had a lot of experience in public speaking. Then I dropped out of college and sang in a band for a couple years. And then I went back to UCLA and got my degree and after I graduated, I got involved in a dot-com company in the early days of the commercial Internet back in 1994. And I ended up being the spokesperson for that company for a few years. That meant that I was going all over the world speaking at conferences. I was on the news, I was on television, I was on radio, and I was in newspapers. I was just constantly speaking at events and to the press. That early career experience ended up becoming what everybody else then wanted me to do for them. So basically, I've been a Chief Evangelist for different tech companies since 1994 and I think that all happened because of my previous public speaking experience in high school and singing in a band for a while.

That's awesome. Great story. A lot of people don't get that opportunity in high school. I wasn't able to speak in front of an audience till later on in life, but being in the military, you had to do that. So that's great. Go ahead.

John Bates: My Dad was a captain in the Marine Corps and there are things I really love about military people, and the first thing which I tell to transitioning vets all the time, is that veterans know how to do something like their life depends on it. And, most people in our society today have no idea what that even means.

That's a true statement, for sure.

John Bates: The other thing I really love about military folks is that they quickly learn that they've got to be gregarious or they're just going to be alone and lonely, you know? Everybody gets moved all over and you have to deal with different people on a regular basis. So I find that military folks are relatively easy to get along with because they just have to adapt that way and I think that's also really cool.

Yes, absolutely. I'm very grateful for what I learned in the military, for sure, and the added benefit once you get down to the civilian world to use those talents.

John Bates: Yes, that's cool. Thank you for that.

Oh, you're welcome. Along the way, was there... Every entrepreneur I've spoken to has had a book that inspired them or helped them. Do you have one that stands out?

John Bates: Well, let's see. I mean there are so many. What's the one I would recommend? Well, you know the one that keeps circling around in my mind right now is... Because I kind of went on a journey that was led by some really good books. One of the books that stand out for me in a big way is a book that some people might even ridicule, but it's brilliant and it's called *"The Secrets of the Millionaire Mind* by T. Harv Eker". T. Harv Eker is a phenomenal presenter and speaker and he does fantastic live events. And his book is short, very easy to read and caused a paradigm shift for me that threw open the doors to a lot more money and a lot more prosperity than I previously had. And, if that's something you want it will work no matter where you are.

And, if you want a book suggestion in the realm of Public Speaking I would highly recommend "Nancy Duarte's" book *"Resonate"*. It's simply fantastic. Another one that is just fabulous is "Craig Valentine's" book *"World Class Speaking"*. He was the 1999 World Champion of Public Speaking with Toastmasters.

Yeah, The Secrets of the Millionaire Mind, that's a great book. I've read that book myself. So that's a good one. You talked about some of these events, and experiences all the way back to high school, tell us about what really gives you the drive and passion for you to help people that you help.

103

John Bates: It comes back to that why statement Simon Sinek helped me develop while I was chilling with him at TEDActive a couple of years ago. I watch people every day. I have a commitment to humanity and one of the ways that I express that is that I genuinely believe, in my heart of hearts, that everyone has something truly awesome to offer this world, no matter what they may think. Some people are really clear that they do have something to offer. Other people think there's no way in the world that they have something to offer and a lot, maybe most people, are somewhere in between. And, I am always looking for that thing somebody has to offer. And crucially, the only way that people get to make a difference in the world is by communicating. If you have a great idea and it just stays in your head forever, then it doesn't make any difference. It could be really nice for you, but it doesn't make any difference for the rest of us. So, what drives me is the ability; is the possibility of bringing out what's truly awesome inside the people that I work with, who are already amazing people, doing amazing things. And I know that there is another level that is possible and I take them to that level. That's what gets me out of bed every day. And I've got to tell you, there's a part of me, my ego part, my negative ego, that on a regular basis will try to make me feel small because I'm not the one who's coming up with the cure for cancer. I'm not the one who found that molecule that will stop Alzheimer's. I'm not on the front line of leading the charge for sustainability, and my little negative ego will say, 'John, you're not actually doing anything. You're just talking to these people who are doing big things.' But the fact of the matter is no matter how wonderful what they're doing is, if they communicate about it even better, it will be multiplied. And that's what I've essentially been doing my whole life. I feel like I've always been a catalyst. There is something here that's happening and when I get added to it, it happens much faster, much better, that kind of catalyst. It is the inspiration of watching the people who are up to big things and wanting to forward their action even more that gives me my energy.

This comes to the next question. You read every day that most people would much rather be in the coffin than delivering the eulogy. And so what's the most common obstacle preventing people from stepping out of their comfort zone, they feel that they've got this message, but they're not quite sure on how to get it out. What's the biggest obstacle preventing them from doing this?

John Bates: Can I give you kind of a two-part answer to that?

Absolutely Of course!

John Bates: A little more than a year ago, right before everything truly went down the tubes in Yemen, my wife and I were invited to go over there to speak and train the speakers at a TEDx event called TEDxTAIZ. And we were terrified. Everybody told us we shouldn't do it, but we went and did it anyway because we wanted to connect with people and make a difference. It was just an unbelievable experience. I'm very glad we did it. And while we were there, we noticed that in Yemen, which is not known for its progressive policies, the organizers were very proud of the fact that they had 50-50 men and women on that stage at TEDxTAIZ. Even though about 50% of the women who were speaking were wearing the full veil, but they still had 50-50 voices represented onstage, and that does not happen in the US and Europe. It's usual that you're lucky if you get 60-40. So, I went back and I asked a bunch of my friends who organize TEDx conferences what that was about, and the simple answer, not necessarily a scientific study, but definitely worth thinking about, surprised me. What they all said in one way or another was, "John, when we ask 10 men to speak, 9 say yes, and when we ask 10 women to speak, 9 say no!" Now, there are a lot of reasons for that. Sometimes the woman is the sole provider of the household income and she's taking care of the kids too and, you know. So there are some good reasons for that. But in my work, what I found, Tracy, was that there are also a lot of really bad reasons for that, which are magnified in women because of our culture, but which are actually an issue for all of us; they're in the way for everyone. So, the number one reason that I've discovered which is, not a good reason that women say no is because they don't think they're enough of an expert yet. They don't want to seem braggy. They don't think they know enough to talk about this to other people. And I'll tell you what, that is a terrible reason to say no and it's actually just a really cheap excuse to get you out of doing something scary. The thing I point out when I speak to women's groups, is the same thing I point out to the people whom I work with that are men, is this: when you say no, you forfeit your opportunity to make a difference. So if you have a really good reason to say no, then say no. But if you say no because you don't think you're enough of an expert, well who are you to tell these people who have invited you to speak that they don't know what they're doing, inviting you to speak? That's silly. That's even a little bit arrogant. So, I think the number one thing that's really in people's way here is this tremendous fear we have of public speaking. Now here's an interesting angle on that, Tracy. It's dangerous to get noticed by the group. It is actually dangerous to be a public speaker. I think evolutionarily, there's a reason we're scared of public speaking, and that is because it's dangerous to get noticed by the group. Look what happened to Jesus and Joan of Arc and Martin Luther King and John F. Kennedy and so on, right?

If people are afraid of public speaking, that is not really the problem. That's actually *good* because if you're not afraid of public speaking at least a little bit, there's a good chance you're a psychopath.

Wow! That's a big jump there.

John Bates: OK, maybe psychopath is strong, but it's fairly scientific. If you're not at least a little bit nervous, then there's something abnormal, actually. I'm smiling, but it's also true. It's typical and normal to be scared. The thing is that *you've got something to say that matters more to you than your fear.* So really, all there is to do is step through it. Acknowledge your fear. Get that it actually makes sense. There's nothing wrong with you. So don't beat yourself up about being scared, just understand that the only way you're going to make a difference is when you get up there and start talking. *If you say no to these engagements, you're missing your opportunity to make a difference.*

Interesting, the women especially suffer from, and I come across this in what I do, this imposter syndrome, where they figure, you know, I'm going to be found out or I'm a charlatan or things like that.

John Bates: Yes. And listen, I've done enough work with people... for the past 13 years plus, I've been coaching people, and everybody's got that. We all have that to some degree or another. If you're self-aware, you've got that a little bit. And I think it's really a shame when people let that stop them. See, this is where my passion really gets engaged. It's because I just know that these people have something to offer and when they say no and they don't offer it, then we're missing out on what they are here to bring to the world.

Yeah, you're actually doing a disservice to the people that you can help for sure.

John Bates: Yes, that's right, but I don't think most people think of it that way because we're all so naturally focused on ourselves. And I will say, Tracy, this brings me to one of the biggest mental jujitsu things that I've been working on lately with the people I train. I love this way of saying it. A friend of mine heard me say this. I would've never even thought about it again, but he captured it and now it's one of my favorite quotes of myself, if it's not too rude of me to quote myself.

No, not at all

John Bates: What I tell people is this: "When you get up onstage, don't worry about what *they* think of *you*. Let *them* know you think *they're* okay." I'll say that one more time. "When you get up onstage, don't worry about what they think of you. Let them know you think they're okay.

"There you go. Beautiful. I like that.

John Bates: It's a fun game to play at a party, too. I've been practicing.

Very nice! Can you describe one of the ways or how you've helped somebody overcome some of those challenges that you just described?

John Bates: Yes. This is a perfect example of the whole thing and it's a woman in this example, but it's not only about women. Her name is Sharon Guynup. She and her partner Steve Winter do a lot of work for *National Geographic*. He's probably the most famous photographer of big cats in the world. He recently got that amazing photograph of the mountain lion in Griffith Park, if you have seen it. And every picture you see of a tiger, big cat lion whatever, that's him. And Sharon and Steve do incredible work together. She's the writer and they are focused on saving big cats in the wild because it's a much bigger problem than anybody even realizes. Tigers and other big cats in the wild are terribly endangered. And, based on the book they were about to release Sharon got an opportunity to speak at TEDxHoboken about 3 years ago and she turned it down because she was so scared. But the organizer called her back and said, look, we've got this speaker coach, he's really good, will you please talk to him because we would really like to have you speak. As I said, she had a book that meant a lot to her coming out, it's called "Tigers Forever" and it's this gorgeous coffee table book and proceeds are going to save the tigers in the wild. So, it mattered to her a lot, but she was so scared she said no, initially. But, she agreed to talk with me and I gave her 2 big things which turned her around. And I'll tell you what I told her, but let me tell you what happened, first. I got an email from her about 6 months or so ago and she said, 'John, I was just thinking of you the other day. And I wanted to tell you thanks because when I met you, I was so scared, I was turning down speaking opportunities. Thank you for working with me. Since working with you and speaking at TEDxHoboken, I've been traveling all over the world and speaking almost every week and I'm *almost* not scared.' So she went from saying no to doing engagements almost every week someplace else in the world talking about what she's passionate about, making a difference in the world because we got her past her fear.

What a great cause helping Big Cats. Getting there message out is important not only through books but speaking as well. Wow! Great story!

John Bates: I'll tell you the 2 things that I did to help her with that if you'd like me to.

Yes, please continue.

John Bates: The first one is that we had that conversation about how it's dangerous to get noticed by the group, as I mentioned. It's natural to be afraid. If you don't want to do it and it's really not worth it to you, then don't do it. But, if it's worth it to you; if you really care about what you're going to go talk

109

about, you're missing your opportunity to make a difference when you say no. And she really got clear about that. It hit her like a ton of bricks because people just don't think about it that way on their own. It's obvious, but it's also very easy to miss. And that made a big difference for her. And then I shared with her what I think is probably the best speaker advice I have ever gotten in my life, and I got it from 2 very different sources, but it is the same basic piece of advice. The first person that I got it from is a guy named Snoop Doggy Dogg. I'm not kidding. And then the second was from one of the top leadership trainers in the world, anywhere outside the military, her name is Candace. And I'll tell you how Snoop Dogg said it first. Snoop Dogg said, very simply, "Don't be nervous. Be at their service."

I like that. Who would have thought that would have come from Snoop Dogg. He is a performer and has done it for quite some time.

John Bates: Which is freaking brilliant, and hilarious. So, Snoop Dogg was the one who began to make the difference for Sharon. Don't be nervous, be at their service. And then the second way, the same thing, same advice but from my trainer who put a little more meat on the bones. She said, 'John, if you get up onstage and you have your attention on yourself,' i.e. you're nervous... because who is nervous about? You! 'If you have your attention on yourself, then you've got your attention on a minor ball of petty concerns that's of no real interest to anyone but you.' Ouch, that hurts, but it's true.

That is another awesome nugget!

John Bates: And then she said, 'However, if you get up onstage and you have your attention on your audience and the difference that you're going to make for them with your message, and the difference they're going to make with the people in their lives because of it, well now you've got your attention on something worth thinking about.'

Beautiful

John Bates: So, don't be nervous, be at their service. And I'm telling you that's all it took. I mean that completely, 180 degrees turned Sharon's life around and she is now out there making the difference that she's committed to making instead of being all upset that she's still saying no to things.

Very good. That's awesome nuggets right there. What would be the first thing that somebody should do if they've got an invite to a TED Talk? I know usually it's not an inexperienced speaker that gets invited. Or if they want to eventually be on a TEDx stage or a TED Talk, what would be the first thing they should do?

John Bates: Well, there are probably 2 questions, maybe in there. If you've already got the invitation, then I would say that it's time for some real soul searching because this is one of those things where you could go pitch your new book or you could go do that talk you always do, all that kind of stuff, but none of that is going to accomplish the real end result that I think you want to accomplish. So, if you've got that invitation to speak at a TEDx, I think the thing to do now is to sit down and really think about this question, and this is a really obvious question, again, but it's something that people find super useful because it's just not something that is obvious when you're sitting in that situation. I ask people, if you had the world's attention for 10, 12, 15 minutes, what's the one idea that you would share with them to make the biggest difference with them? What is that one thing that you would say if you knew the world was really going to listen? What would you tell them?

Nice. I like that.

John Bates: Great, I'm glad you do, because it seems pretty obvious when you hear it but it's always fun to watch people's eyes light up when you say it and they hadn't quite thought of it that way yet.

Yeah, and it becomes, it actually becomes easy when you break it down like that and you can open the fear and you start internalizing what you're going to say.

John Bates: Yes. This is why I think all of my initial work doing TED and TEDx things has translated so incredibly well. I mean surprisingly to me, very happily surprisingly well, my wife and I are pinching each other on a daily basis. We say, 'Really? Oh my God! Really?' And we're just thrilled and happy and appreciative and grateful. And I think that this is why that work with TED and TEDx translates so well to the corporate world and to the leadership world because I think if I were to boil down the formula that goes into creating a good TED Talk, it's very much the same formula that goes into any great communication, and I think communication and leadership are inextricably entwined. So, what are your intentions? Because a lot of times, people don't take their time to ask themselves what is my intention with this communication. I didn't use to do that. I didn't even *think* about the fact that I had an intention with my communication. I just opened my mouth and blabbed, until it was pointed out to me. Thank God for Candace and all the other people who cared enough to drag me to consciousness, as I often kicked and screamed and resisted. Anyway, when people really asked what is the intention, and then when they really focus, things start to happen. Then add the fact that the real core of a TED Talk is that one idea. It can't be your 3 or 4 ideas. It's got to be very targeted and focused because it's such a short period of time and you want to have the maximum impact. So what's the intention, what's the main idea, what's that one thing you really want to land over there, and then what are you really committed to accomplishing? If you really think about it, is this communication forwarding the action of what you're genuinely committed to, or is it not?

I think the TED Talks have given it a label. And created it as such a value. You can say that you're a keynote speaker, but then you can say, well, I spoke, I'm a TED Talk speaker. It takes on a whole different perspective.

John Bates: Yes, it sure does. Now, the whole TEDx event thing is a little uneven. It's kind of like pro-football versus college football or even sometimes high school football. But I just think it's been wonderful, it's great that this whole thing has been given a label, essentially, and been recognized as something so worthwhile.

It's a whole different standard, for sure. That's great content. And then it's kind of working backwards into corporate America, where hey, we're going to set this standard within the corporation of people that are communicating with our employees. And this is what we want. So that's good stuff. I love how that's going.

John Bates: Me too.

Absolutely, you've got it. And, I teach this concept; micro-specialized, and you're certainly micro-specialized in helping those folks. How can the reader find out more about how to get involved with you or find out about your services? What do they need to do?

John Bates: Well, the main thing, I think, is just my website, which is www.executivespeakingsuccess.com. And I also have a very affordable online e-course. You can go to atspeaking.executivespeakingsuccess.com, which gives anyone access to the same basic training that we work with at top companies rave about. I'm very happy to have the possibility of contributing more broadly with that vehicle.

Awesome so if somebody wants to immediately contact you, do you have a phone number or an email address that they can get a hold of you?

John Bates: Yes, So my number is +1 (424) 234-1063 and then my email. You know I think what I'll do is I'll set one up that's john.bates@executivespeakingsuccess.com just so I can tell where it came from.

Great service and looking forward to a future relationship, for sure.

John Bates: Likewise, likewise. Thank you, Tracy. I really appreciate your time.

You bet. I'll talk to you soon. Thank you.

WEBSITE:
www.speaking.executivespeakingsuccess.com
www.atspeaking.executivespeakingsuccess.com

EMAIL:
john.bates@executivespeakingsuccess.com

LINKEDIN:
https://www.linkedin.com/in/johnbates

FACEBOOK:
https://www.facebook.com/therealjohnkbates

PHONE:
(424) 234-1063

An Entrepreneur Driven to Make a Mark

Hotel and Event Management

Pritesh is a passionate and grateful entrepreneur that loves to interact with people, take on huge challenges, and dares to dream. He is determined to be better today than yesterday and better tomorrow than today. Driven on self-development and self-mastery when it comes to his craft, his business, and most importantly himself. A believer in karma and how thoughts, beliefs, and how the past, current, and future actions determine energies around oneself. Devoted to hard work, mind management and self-transformation. Drawn to the creative, unique, and those willing to shape and be shaped by the world. Constantly motivated to overcome fears, doubts and on a mission to prove the limitless nature of the universe.

Pritesh realized that he did not want to work for a corporation or in an environment that would not give him the freedom to reach his highest potential. Working as an IT Consultant from 2001 - 2008 he was not satisfied with the way his career and life were moving. Pritesh was not able to develop deep relationships, and was not able to get up every morning excited to work, and he felt he was not living the life he would be satisfied with. He was not being utilized for his calling. Pritesh was in a search and in that search, he found entrepreneurship.

His father was a successful entrepreneur in the financial lending industry. During his time in college, he required that he spend his free time between classes and after school in the back of his office. During his time in college, his father required that Pritesh spend his free time between classes and after school in the back of his office. He wanted Pritesh to observe him, learn the art of negotiating, and understand the importance of building relationships with clients. In that office, Pritesh dreamed of one day sitting in a position of influence as did his father. Coming from a successful father, he always had the confidence that he needed to lead a whole life. He learned from a very early age that to achieve his highest desires, it required continual self-motivation, big dreams and courage to take risks.

Hard work, persistence, dedication, curiosity, and a good intention was his drive when he was a green entrepreneur. Pritesh sacrificed his time with himself, with his wife, with his family and social circles to develop his business. He has worked 18 to 20 hour days, attempted to learn every job responsibility required to operate a hotel, in order to create best practices, know his product, standardize processes, and develop great people. Through his experiences, he has learned that by optimizing the 3 P's: Product, Process, and People he can achieve the 4th P: Profit. He is surrounded by great mentors and

117

teachers. One of his business partners has been in the Food & Beverage industry for 30 years. To learn from him, he asked him to teach him the ins and outs of the banquet business. On a night they were hosting a wedding reception for 650 guests, his business partner told all the five dishwashers to go home early that night. He looked at Pritesh and said" "You want to learn this business right?" As he says that, he takes off his suit blazer, rolls up his shirt sleeves and starts to wash the dishes and looks over to him to do the same. They washed all the dishes that night. Pritesh learned that every position is critical to the success of an operation, and all levels of employment must be respected and commended for their contribution. No great business can be built without a dedicated; goal oriented and well managed team.

He realized he was an entrepreneur when opportunities to help and influence others started to show up continually. When he was looked upon for solutions, guidance, motivation, advice, and contribution, he knew he found his calling.

Conversation with Pritesh Ghandhi

Tell me about your business, your business name, and the types of customers you help. Basically, describe the clients you help.

Pritesh Gandhi: I'm the co-owner of the Clarion Inn Hotel & Waterford Banquets in Elmhurst, IL. We specialize in organizing corporate conferences, seminars, weddings, social parties and providing lodging for our guests. Our business has many different customer segments. When it comes to weddings - we have hosted all different religious ceremonies, but primarily the bulk of our business is South Asian weddings, which are "the Big Fat Indian weddings" you hear about. They're full of color, amazing clothing, grooms that arrive on horses, exotic cars, and helicopters, entertainment that feature fireworks, Bollywood dance performances, and couples that host multiple day events that average 400-600 guests. These types of events require detailed event management, large volumes of hotel lodging, and ethnic multi-cuisine meals.

We were recently featured on the front page of the Chicago Tribune. The article was about the growth of the Indian population in Chicago land and how vendors servicing the wedding industry are flourishing. Our business was featured in the article as the premier venue to host an Indian wedding. We pride ourselves on the high service levels, knowledge of the South Asian culture, and convenience to guests as we have both conference space and hotel rooms all in one location. We host over 100 south Asian Wedding annually and each one has its own unique challenges and intricacies.

We're in the hospitality industry; therefore there is never a boring day.

That's perfect. I teach entrepreneurs how to micro-specialize, so you've got a pretty awesome niche right there, so that's great.

What led you to this field, and how did you get started in this business?

Pritesh Gandhi: It starts at home. My father was an immigrant, came here in 1970. It's the American Dream type of story. He came to the states to make something of his life, arrived as the first member of his family - in an effort to make a positive contribution. He came to this country for education, got into Stanford and couldn't afford it, and ended up attending smaller universities where he earned a Masters and an MBA. Through hard work, persistence, and a dynamic personality he had some opportunity breaks and became a very successful entrepreneur himself. He laid the path for me and my two sisters; he sponsored his family to migrate from India to the US, and made this country his home. He has made many sacrifices in his life for the betterment of his family.   Though he couldn't afford it, he moved our family into the suburbs where I received the greatest education.   Education has always been a foundational pillar he stressed to me and my sisters.

While I was in college, my father discouraged me to get a job off campus.. He preferred I sit in the back of his office. He said, "You know, I don't want you to waste time fooling around in college. Just come to my office as soon as you have gaps between your classes. I want you to sit in the back and just listen in, and have a laptop open." He set a professional tone for me from an early age. I didn't know what he was doing. He was in the finance industry at that time, and a commercial lender. He would have all different types of entrepreneurs and small business owners come to him for lending. He wanted me to absorb the art of negotiating, the art of customer relationship, and the importance of creating connections with people. I didn't know what this experience was paving for me at that time.

Then when I finished college I had a dual degree in Finance and Informational Decision Sciences. I was the valedictorian of my class in college; had a perfect GPA. I worked in corporate

America for 8 years, moved up the ranks, but I was not able to fulfill my dreams, build strong relationships, nor was I happy. I started to think about those days I spent in my father's office - where he talked to real people, helped small business owners, and was part of something really local and organic. I realized the importance of the time I had spent in his office during my college years.

I reached back out to him and said, "Hey, I'm not satisfied with what I'm doing for a living, and it's taking a toll on my happiness," and I said, "Look out for an opportunity for me, something challenging and something that could be my own." He came across a failed hotel property that needed a lot of TLC - tender loving care. I looked at it, and thought it's a huge challenge and something that I could see myself completely diving into. It was my opportunity to develop something from infancy and create my legacy.

My father introduced me to two other entrepreneurs that became my partners, mentors, and essentially great influencers in my life. One of my partners has a background of developing hotels for the past 25 years and another partner that has been in the food and beverage industry for 30 years. My quest for greatness had started a journey with a group of men that took me under their wings and gave me the confidence to grow into a leader in the hospitality and service industry.

Fortunately in the process of taking this bold risk, I found my passion, which was awesome. I found it in many, many facets, which one was in sales. Being in sales has allowed me to earn people's trust, develop long standing relationships, experience the joys of winning accounts, and also utilize my negotiation skills. Sales brought out a healthy competitive nature that I had lost in my corporate job.

Leadership was another great passion that I found in my entrepreneurial journey. I currently lead over 65 employees. I have learned that by coaching and mentoring others you get to learn a lot about yourself.

The ability to interact with people from all different backgrounds is the best part of my job. I have the pleasure to lead diverse groups of people that all have valuable perspectives. I also have the pleasure to meet a lot of interesting people that come through our doors. I get to witness clients host their memorable life events such as weddings, baby showers, birthdays and anniversary parties. I meet people from all around the world that travel, share their stories and experiences. Things kind of fell in place for me and it is just amazing. Coming into entrepreneurship has allowed me to work at the ground level where things are still very human.

Very nice, that's a very, very good explanation of how you got into it and the back story, and I appreciate you sharing that with me. Every entrepreneur I speak to has something that inspired them along the way in the form of a book or a movie? Is there one book that stands out that helped you?

Pritesh Gandhi: Yes. The book that really inspired me was The Power of Intention by Wayne Dyer. I read this book in my mid 20s. I was in dire search of happiness. I didn't know if I was going to find solutions in a book to get my hunger back but I was desperate. I could not express what I was looking for to others and get them to understand me. I didn't know if I was going through depression or just really lost. I was trying to figure myself out. I felt like I was not living to my maximum potential.

The book the Power of Intention brought to light that there is a higher power out there that wants you to do what you're intended to do. The focused mind is your greatest ally to create the life you intend to live. This focused intention allows the Universe to move things towards your truest and highest intentions. I was enlightened to listen to my intuition, dared to follow my heart versus the money, and continually checking to make sure I take actions that make me most happy. It also brought out the importance of thought power and how a clear mind can make your desired life appear.

Good stuff, Talk about what makes you get up out of bed every morning. What's that passion that you have to help others?

Pritesh Gandhi*:* I'm blessed to have a platform where many people can come together to do great work or celebrate accomplishments or life's milestones.

I have a platform, a stage here, and every day our clients come to our facility to create synergies, innovate and improve. We are a service provider that can facilitate the flow of things in our world. This is the reason I'm hungry to get up every morning. We are an instrument being used to create a positive impact in the world.

I'm very passionate about being a small business owner in the hospitality and service industry. Small businesses are the lifeblood of the economy. We employee, we sacrifice, we work our tails off and we have a fire within us to add value to the world.

You mentioned your target audience and who you help. What are some of the most common obstacles that target audience, that's preventing them from having a successful event here in the United States or, what are some of the obstacles?

Pritesh Gandhi: A big wedding has the perfect recipe for disaster: obstacles include high emotions, many opinions, rituals, different levels of expectations, multiple families, high levels of stress, and all sorts of requirements such as food and beverage, lodging and transportation. Plus, you're working with many vendors: florists, decorators, DJs, live bands, food caterers, photographers, videographers, and hair and makeup stylists.

These events require a tremendous amount of experience, coordination, knowledge, attention to detail, patience, and project management skills. It's just a lot of moving parts, and you need somebody that understands the families, understands what their needs are, how flawless things have to be, how important it is that things get done correctly and in a timely manner.

How can the reader avoid some of these things that you just described, and how can they overcome them? You can do this by telling an actual event, how you helped someone with their event. Maybe they had a challenge and then you helped them overcome it during that particular event with a client.

Pritesh Gandhi: In the hospitality and service industry you need the right people. Nothing can happen with one person doing everything. You need a solid group of people that are focused to achieve greatness. Our people are our assets!

One of my mottos is "Come to work if you're ready to serve others." That's the thing that people forget, that yes, we're in the service industry, but they don't understand what that truly means. That means that you are setting your egos aside, and you're passionate about helping and serving others. That's the purpose of the industry that we're in. Everything on a daily basis only works when the team is in sync and they're motivated, and they're behind common goals, and they're passionate about what they do.

I have learned that to achieve greatness, you have to focus on improvements across your product, your processes, and your people. Obviously, leadership is huge, and it's not just me leading, it's also creating leaders at every level of your organization. That's one of the greatest things that people don't know that they have this leadership quality that they can develop, and how much gratification they can get from teaching people, and mentoring them.

Perfect. Do you remember a group that came to you that was a challenge and you pulled it off? Do you have a recollection of that?

Pritesh Gandhi: One of the biggest challenges we had was a bride that was high-demanding, high maintenance, and had a very complicated menu. She wanted a complete vegan menu for a 350 guest Indian wedding.

We worked very closely with the chef to develop a custom menu that would not impact quality, taste, texture, and presentation.

It took a lot of creativity, collaboration, and feedback to successfully pull off this event. In the service industry, "There's no such thing as a NO." It's just your willingness to take on something new and challenging. It's your ability to provide solutions and see opportunities in obstacles.

That's an awesome example. It's like Branson says, "If a customer asks you if you can do it, and if you can't, you say, "Yes," and figure it out."

Pritesh Gandhi: *Yeah, exactly.*

Very good, what's the first thing that the reader should do if they're considering having an event as you described? It's not necessarily traditional. What would be the first thing they should do?

Pritesh Gandhi: First thing that I think a wedding couple should do is know the importance of their wedding from a significance point of view. It's the day that loved ones are present to witness a special occasion in their lives, provide support and give them blessings. If you keep your mind on that, it could make your experience of planning a wedding a lot easier and may remove the tension. Every couple should also consider injecting their personalities into their events. Tell a story about themselves from the party favors, themes, décor, menu, and their entertainment. This will differentiate their wedding from all the others.

Excellent nuggets there, If somebody's ready to get started, if they want to find out more about how you can help them with their special event, how can they find out more?

Pritesh Gandhi*: Go to www.waterfordbanquet.com and www.clarionInnelmhurst.com. They can find us on Facebook and find me on LinkedIn*

Yeah, that should be one ... How can they reach you, if they're ready to start now, how can they reach you by phone or email?

Pritesh Gandhi*:* Yeah, sure. Its PriteshGandhi90@gmail.com, or they could call me at my phone number 630-279-0270, extension 3. I could give you my cell phone too, 847-791-1553.

Perfect. That concludes our interview. You did a great job. Lots of great nuggets Thanks again for participating.

WEBSITE:
http://www.WaterfordBaquet.com
http://www.ClarionInnElmhurst.Com

EMAIL:
priteshgandhi90@gmail.com

LINKEDIN:
http://www.linkedin.com/in/priteshgandhi90

PHONE:
(847) 791-1553

Active Enterprises Inc.
(DBA Anytime Fitness)

Helping People Get to a Healthier Place in Life

James read the book "Rich Dad, Poor Dad" by Robert Kiyosaki in 2010 about the same time he was getting sick of his corporate job moving him to areas he didn't want to live. After reading that book, James purchased 3 Anytime Fitness territories, created Active Enterprises Inc., left the corporate job and swung for the fences.......and he made contact and hit it out of the park!

About a week after he opened his first business, James' business partner (who happened to be his fiancée at the time) decided to quit Active Enterprises Inc. and leave him, not only with some difficult emotions, but also with having to deal with a start-up business solo along with her responsibilities of the business plan, and his personal plans. At the time, he felt like he was being buried alive, but he kept focusing on a day at a time with the business and had no other choice but to learn all facets of the business because he was the only hope to keep paying the SBA loan. Looking back, that was the best thing for him, as James started his 2nd business, and he currently is working on opening a 3rd business as well as some other ventures, he is no longer near as scared and nervous. He went on to say "Life's about the view through your windshield. Have a vision and set goals. Always ask how, never say can't and live and love what you do. You know, live it and love it! Sounds cliché, but what doesn't kill you makes you stronger, experience is the best teacher and the cup is always half full. Follow these rules and chances are, life will be epic!"

Conversation with James Adamitis

Thanks for being a part of the book project James. Go ahead and tell us about your business and what types of customers you help.

JAMES ADAMITIS: My business is a franchise that you have a lot of autonomy with how you run it. It's a fitness business, a gym, but more than just the sign-up of a member and on to the next sign-up mentality that most gyms operate by, we are really focused on trying to help people get to a healthier place in life regarding their overall wellness. We truly want them to get to a healthier place in life all around, from their physical attributes of looking better and healthier, to the mental side of being more positive and clear headed, to also being healthy on the inside with your organs, cholesterol, diabetes and overall in fit shape. We also help anyone who comes off an injury once their physical therapy is complete and they need to continue to gain strength and improve. We do not offer physical therapy, but as soon as they are cleared, we can take over with teaching and helping them with exercise and habits to keep on a successful non-injury path in the future. Overall, we are a full-service gym, offering healthy supplements, personal and small group training and group classes, etc. What makes us #1 in our market, is that we service our customers and most really need it. I'm getting ready to open a second club, will be my first in California which will be an entirely different demographic. My demographic in Central Kentucky (where my first gym is located) has a 33% obesity rate, so we are targeting a lot of people that have never exercised or have ever used our services/products before. It takes a lot of convincing with our customer base that not only do they need to start being active and healthy and change their lifestyle, but they also have to, and then we have to hammer home why they need to do it. For some, it will eventually become a matter of life or death. It's a different demographic in Central KY from what I was used to being around growing up and also where I lived most of my career. I tell people that when we're working on the gym plan out in California, it's not a matter of if the base customer exercises, it's a matter of when they exercise; it is part of the lifestyle, and that is what I was used to.....you know, working out is just another "to-do" on the daily list. With our demographic in Central Kentucky, it's a matter of if they exercise at all. Some people have never seen a gym or even walked in one before, which again, is a different demographic that I was used to growing up and being around when I traveled in my career. So servicing people that need our services and products, but they don't think they need us at times, makes our job a challenge. You almost have to want it for the customer more than they want it for themselves.

Right. Well, that's interesting because I talk about people that are positioned in their field as the experts, and I always mention Richard Simmons and his target audience is not P90X people but middle-aged women that, you know, hardly can get up off the couch and things like that. So you have to be aware of those target niches and areas of the country that you're in when you're opening these gyms. So, what led you to this field and how did you get started in this business?

JAMES ADAMITIS: Well, I was working in a completely different business. I was in alcohol sales with the #1 global beer company in the world. I had been promoted from living in Southern California to Texas, then eventually expanded to North Louisiana. At that point, I was getting frustrated of being re-located for promotions to places that I didn't necessarily want to live or even ever had thought of living. I always took the promotion for the obvious financial reasons, more money, but the money never made me as happy as I expected it would. Having just read the book, "Rich Dad, Poor Dad" by Robert Kiyosaki, and it being around year seven of my career, I began to get into the entrepreneur mindset. He struck a chord with me about how I grew up with teachers. Both of my parents are teachers. They were great, wouldn't trade them for the world and are the reason I have success today and had a great education. In comparison to the book, though, they were the "poor dad." The message was get a good education, then a good job with a big company, have a long career, then retire happy. At the point I was in my career and having read that book, I had already been feeling that maybe a move and change needed to be made. I remember going into liquor stores and trying to price our low priced malt liquor single serve items into the price range where people who were on welfare could afford it, and that was a strategy for some markets and stores. This wasn't all the time, but this was one of the moments that had me starting to think, "What am I doing?" Am I helping out the world? Am I doing what I want to do? I had also joined a new gym at this point that was different from any other gym I had ever joined. It was called Anytime Fitness, and it was the only 24-hour gym that was available in Louisiana at that time. While traveling and working out at these gyms, I really loved their concept. It was great how I could work out wherever I was for businesses, even when in very rural areas and have 24-hour access. Besides not having a pool and a steam room, these clubs had all the equipment I used 95% of the time. It all started coming together. I thought this looked like it could be affordable. I had a pretty healthy 401-K at that point, some savings, an excellent credit rating and a passion for fitness. I had always loved working out, had exercised consistently since I was 14, and that's where the light bulb came on. I started talking to the managers at these clubs and found out the business was affordable and like most, it was about finding the right location to make them successful. I was about to be 30 and was in the 30-year old mind phase of, if a change is going to happen, it probably needs to happen soon. I thought I have to do something else in life. It's either going to be, move around, chasing promotions to different cities where my corporate company wanted me to live and doing the work that sometimes I didn't find rewarding, or, I just could go all in and completely change up the game to do something I was passionate about, and that's what happened. I decided at that point that I was going to try to make a living off of something that I was passionate about. Right? I will profit off of my passion. That's really what I thought was the way to go, and that's exactly what happened.

That's a great story. Thanks for sharing that. I interview lots of entrepreneurs, and there is always something along the way, that inspired them, was there somebody in particular or maybe a book or movie that also inspired you?

JAMES ADAMITIS: Well, obviously, the book *Rich Dad, Poor Dad* by Robert Kiyosaki. That was the one that made me want to be an entrepreneur and be a businessman. Get in the business owner quadrant. I had been in the employee quadrant my whole life, with my long term 401k and Roth IRA being in the investor quadrant, but I wanted to exit the employee quadrant into the business owner quadrant, having more control of my money and time. That was a big influence. Also, seeing how hard my parents worked as teachers, especially in their later years having to work a lot of hours at their age and seeing how hard that was for them. Then seeing how my friends' parents who were business owners, that took some big financial risks around the age I was thinking about doing this, was motivation as well. I saw how the business owners were living and how they sometimes were outside on the golf course having a cigar, or traveling to exotic places and living what seemed like their dream made me want to gravitate to that side. For my dream, it would be to have a little fun on a Friday afternoon or even sleep in a little on a Monday, rather than work all Friday or be up bright and early on Monday. So, that's how it started inspiring me. Reading that book and thinking about the comparisons of growing up with great parents who gave me an excellent education, but also seeing those parents that had a business background have it a little easier with more discretionary income. It was not just one person individually who inspired me. It was a mix of all of the above that caused me to change up the gears.

Nice. It seems to be the book for all the entrepreneurs that I speak to. They mention that book, so that's awesome book to reference for sure. The problem or the most common obstacle preventing the people that you describe, or the people you're targeting, what is the biggest obstacle to preventing them from doing the things they need to do to get in shape or have a healthier lifestyle?

JAMES ADAMITIS: I think one factor is having a positive mindset. One, the cup is always half-full. I think when we all wake up every day, we have a choice to choose to be happy. I think that's a tough thing for some people to understand that they have the option to turn their mind in a particular direction. I think some people have let go of themselves physically for so long that they come in with a great passion. Maybe they just woke up and finally decided, "I'm sick of being this big, or this unhealthy." Or a doctor says, "Hey, you've got to go exercise", but then once they join and start the work and get discouraged because they worked their butt off for two weeks and nothing happens. At that stage is where the biggest obstacles start. We try to coach our members that it's a one a day a time mentality; there will be struggles and that they didn't get unhealthy overnight. So the obstacle comes in changing their mindset and like I stated above, sometimes wanting it more for them than they want it for themselves. I try to use and teach the KISS method in life: Keep it simple, starter. Try to keep things as simple as possible when starting something new and know as long as you're doing the daily goals and the baby steps to your goals, not making them more complicated than needed, you'll eventually attain them. Another obstacle we have is that we don't sell month-to-month memberships, and we are not the cheapest gym in town. To join our club, a one-year membership is required. We don't mess with month-to-month membership because what happens is, if someone does a month-to-month contract, they'll quit after a month 90% of the time because they will give up on themselves. But once you give them the yearly minimum of a membership during sign up and explain that if they are committed to getting to a healthier place and in some cases, it took them over a year to get in the condition they are in, they usually sign up. Then if they get discouraged, it's like, okay you're in it for a year, now let's take it a day at a time and KISS. You are in it for the next year, can't cancel so let's finish what we started. So our obstacles come in trying to get them signed up for commitment, then keeping their mindset positive with small goals for the long-term outcome.

How do you get them over that, or how do you fix their mindset? How do you counsel them, or coach them in that regard?

James Adamitis: We hold them accountable in a nice way by setting out different types of tracking systems that reward people for good participation and incentivize them to compete and participate. We do a monthly top 10 of the top 10 members who have used the club the prior month. We call it "Gym Junkies" and post it in our monthly newsletter, on all social media pages and a big wall in the gym. That gets a lot of people excited having their name on the board, in social media and in the club newsletter. We reward the first "gym junkie" with a prize like a free shirt, discount a month of membership or something to make them want to be #1 on the list. So we are incentivizing them with recognition and small prizes. We also do member spotlight stories which help motivate our members. For the most part, our demographic, mainly wants to lose weight, so we tend to have member spotlight stories every month where we'll target people that had lost weight if they needed help when they started. We'll try members who have trained with our trainers, because not only will it help get the trainers recognition which may open up more opportunity for more clients, typically 95% of the people who are in our training program don't quit the gym. They don't stop training because they see results, and they're with a professional. So we'll do one member every month that has reached a goal, and that helps inspire to say, well if this person was that big and they lost all that weight, or on occasion if this person was built like a toothpick and now looks ripped and healthy, then I can do it. Lastly, we also place people who have trained with our program and their story of success, achieving their goals on a wall that is like the "Training Hall of Fame". So they're always up there as long as they're a member, and they have that moment in their gym history for them to feel proud about. It's there for newer members to see and inspire and also for those who are on the wall to see and hopefully keep them motivated to continue. This also helps market our training program.

Yes, most people like recognition for sure, and that's a big motivator, so that's excellent. Could you describe how you helped someone or helped one of your clients achieve the success of being in shape or losing weight or bulking up?

James Adamitis: I've been in sales most of my life and the overall jest of a sale, is all about knowing your audience (the customer). Blueprint what you think the customer needs. Uncover what the customer says they need. Support what the business can do for what you feel the customer needs as well as what they feel they need. Collaborate with the customer and combine the business support with their needs. "Handshake" and ask for the sale, then close the sale. This was how I approached one of my members. She came in and was near 400 lbs. honestly, one of the biggest people I had ever seen in person. I was in my early 30s at the time and thought she was in her 40s; she was in her late 20s. So off the bat, I knew she needed a significant lifestyle change. Her doctor told her she needed to exercise, diet, etc. She had type 2 diabetes, high blood pressure, and high cholesterol. After going through everything in our process of signing members up, she said we were too expensive and that she was going to look at other places. As she walked out, I had this feeling that she would die if she didn't join my club. I knew no other club in town would care about her like we would. I ended up running out the door, bringing her back inside and striking a deal with her on a price below what I typically would offer if she promised to meet with my training manager and, at least, go through a fitness consultation. My hope was during that she would learn more about what she needed to do in order to get healthy. And although we lost the price point I budgeted, maybe she would sign up for training and not only help offset some of the money we lost on the membership, more importantly, she would be able to lose the weight needed. Knowing her needs, etc. from the fact finding process, I let my Personal Training Manager know the trainer she would do well with if she signed up for training as well as the price points we could work with her on and how many times a month she needed to stay on the path. Well, she ended up signing up for training and one year later had lost 190 lbs., met a boyfriend, got engaged and had a baby. If I had not made the extra effort that day, scary to think where she would be today. So I treated her as an individual person, not a number as a lot of gyms and am jubilant with the outcome.

Yes, people can get lost in full gym scenarios and become a number, so that's awesome that you treat each person as an individual and cater to their needs.

James Adamitis: Yes, a lot of gyms, especially low-cost gyms, could care less about the member once they sign the contract. Any gym that charges you $20 or less a month and offers month-to-month agreements only wants lots of members, and they want those members not to use the club because they need a ton of members to stay in business, and if all of them use the club, equipment will break down quickly. Since they are so concerned with the next sale, they don't take the time with new members or current members to know their needs and them as a person. We may cost more than most gyms in our area, but we will know your name, your goals and you will get results. The whole point of joining a gym is RESULTS!

What would be the best piece of advice that you would give someone who's considering participating in a gym membership or finding the right gym to meet their needs?

James Adamitis: What's the best piece of advice I can give them? I would say, first off, do your homework. So definitely, draw a line. Find out exactly where the gyms are located to where you live. The number one thing is the convenience, right? If you don't have a gym that's near where you work or where you live, you're probably not going to use it that often. We've got a lot of people that like the $10 a month gym that's 30 minutes away from us. Yeah it's a great deal, but they never go and then we see a lot of them come our way and think we are pricy, but once they join, they always are happier with us. So, convenience is the one the thing I tell them. Make sure you have something that's convenient, and that makes sense regarding your geographic area. Two, do your homework in terms trying the club. Most clubs will let you try them for at least a couple days to a week. We offer seven days and on occasion 14-day trials. Also, after trying the club, you should know the pricing and make sure it is in your budget. If you make $30,000 a year, you probably shouldn't join a $200 a month club. Check out the club web-site and read reviews on Yelp, Facebook, Google, etc. Find out what their customers are saying about the club and talk to members of the organization to know if they are getting the results and achieving their goals. And make sure that if you're interested in personal training, the club has excellent certified trainers, preferably trainers who have a college degree or some college experience with Exercise Science, Kinesiology, Biology, some of those majors that can help give you the best knowledge and advice while you train. Some trainers have nutrition education as well which is always a plus! So overall, do your homework on convenience, try the club, seek reviews/referrals and then know your budget and you will be okay.

I notice recently in the news or people write about, there's a discussion about cardio versus weight-lifting and people think that 30 minutes of riding a bike or doing a treadmill is not sufficient. Could you elaborate on that a little bit more?

James Adamitis: Well, I'm a gym owner, not a certified personal trainer, so this is probably a question better for my trainers to answer, but there's a theory that I agree with that you can do strength training as your cardio simultaneously. Most of the time when I exercise it is more of a fast-paced circuit strength training workout. So rather than be on a bike for 30 minutes to keep your heart rate up, you can do a chest, bicep, and a core circuit all in a row for 30 minutes. Always exercising, only taking small breaks in between each set while still keeping up a constant heart rate for your cardio, which is going to, in turn, burn fat and also build muscle mass. Killing two birds with one stone, if that makes sense. That's how my trainers have trained me, and that's the way I work out now. I like to run on the beach and outdoors, but if I'm pressed for time and only have 45 minutes to work out, I'm going to choose no cardio through a bike/treadmill and will do the cardio with strength training.

Okay, so it makes a lot of sense, then, to do it that way. How can a reader find out more about you and how they could get started with you?

James Adamitis: You can find me individually on LinkedIn as James Adamitis (Los Angeles area) and Twitter j_adam_it_is. You can find my fitness center on Facebook at www.Facebook.com/AnytimeFitnessNicholasville. There are a lot of good details on that site about the gym in Kentucky. The gym's Instagram and Twitter are @anytimenville for the club as well. If you go to www.AnytimeFitness.com, that will give you access to the network of organizations around the world owned and operated by other owners. I also am an executive producer on a documentary about the academy award winning director of iconic films such as "Rocky" and "Karate Kid," called "John G. Avildsen: King of the Underdogs." It will be released in 2016, and we have Sylvester Stallone, Martin Scorsese, and other houses hold names in the film. Lastly, I own a start-up clothing line called 70andSunny. You can find out more at www.70andSunny.com.

Great. Are there any videos or any information there for them to download or to look at?

James Adamitis: For the gym, we have a YouTube channel, just search Anytime Fitness Nicholasville on YouTube and you will find our channel. It has exercise videos with trainers, a tour of our club and all kinds of different stuff on the channel.

Perfect. If somebody's ready to get started right now can they call you or e-mail you? How can they do that?

James Adamitis: Oh yeah! My email is james.adamitis@anytimefitness.com and is the best email to get in contact with me. And even if I don't have a gym in their area, I could put them in contact with somebody who does and give them the proper contact to get started. We have over 2,000 clubs between Canada and the U.S.A. I'm well connected with many owners and the corporate office so I could point them in the right direction.

Perfect. Well, this concludes our interview and thank you very much for the great information.

James Adamitis: No problem. Thank you!

WEBSITE:

http://anytimefitness.com/gyms/2540/nicholasville-ky-40356
http://70andSunny.com

EMAIL:

james.adamitis@anytimefitness.com

FACEBOOK:

https://www.facebook.com/JamesRAdamitis

LINKEDIN:

https://www.linkedin.com/in/jamesadamitis

YOUTUBE:

https://www.youtube.com/channel/UCMh8N_oYsyqE33De1SVWgCg

PHONE:

(859) 550-3338

Media Coach & Public Speaking Trainer

Media Expert Re-Writing her Future Producing the Best You

Kathryn is a three time Emmy award winning media expert. She worked in TV newsrooms across the country and was a spokesperson for a law enforcement agency.

For years, she dreamed about starting her own company. When she was laid off from a now defunct television network – it was the push she needed to kick her into entrepreneurialism.

143

Kathryn is now a media coach/strategist and a public speaking trainer for corporations and individuals across the world. She still produces TV shows and other video for clients who need her expertise. She also mentors college students and is on the advisory board for a charity that sends U.S. military veteran families to college.

The most important piece she looks for in clients is the desire to improve themselves. One of the first questions she asks when someone's staff calls her for help is: "Do they WANT this? Do they want to be the best? Are they able to change in order to stand out?"

If the answer is YES — she's all in.

Conversation with Kathryn Janicek

Kathryn, thanks again for joining us today. Let's just get right into it. Tell us about your business, your business name and what types of customers you help.

I've won three Emmys for breaking news and social media – and two Associated Press awards. I've been in media for almost twenty years. I have worked in cities across the United States as a TV news executive producer, producer, VP of news for a national network and a spokesperson for law enforcement.

My career sent me to seven cities in less than 15 years – and when it was time for me to make my next jump a few years ago – it meant moving to LA or NY to move up and make more money. After moving around so much for my career and as a child (5 elementary schools & 3 high schools) – I really wanted to stay close to family and continue building my network in Chicago. And why not? Besides the taxes, Chicago is the perfect city. Culture – theater – strong work ethic – restaurants – great neighborhoods... it could be the best city in the country. So it was time for me to figure out what was next without moving.

The problem was, I didn't think I had skills that were translatable to another career. What exactly did I do? I wanted to leverage all the knowledge I had soaked up over the years. I knew how to produce television, lead anchors, reporters and a team of producers and writers. I juggled live shots, a chopper and kept the weather guy talking when a story needed a few more seconds before it was ready to make air. I knew what was important for my viewers to learn, what was trending, how to dig up a story... how to train people on how to write news for TV, web and radio... but at the time, I didn't know how to create a company out of those talents.

As it turned out, I didn't have to. Once I became a free agent - people reached out asking for help. They told *me* what they needed.

"I could use help with media strategy."

"I want to get better at delivering big speeches."

"I want to know what to wear and what to do with my hands on stage."

"I want to get into the media. I want my fifteen minutes. I want free publicity."

"I want my story out there."

"My client needs a media coach."

"I want to sell more."

"Can you help me?"

That's how I started Kathryn Janicek Productions.

I guide organizations in media strategy and public speaking training. I coach executives looking to move up in their career, those who are making major speeches for the first or 100th time -- and spokespeople who need to get "media ready." They need help delivering a more memorable message, and I produce that for them. I also coach people who speak English as their second or third language – helping them with delivery, pronunciation, vocabulary, cultural things... whatever they need.

Some clients have wanted to be on TV – or be seen as an expert in their field – but they need help getting their story out of them. I guide them on what a writer or producer may find interesting about them... and then coach them on how to perform better when it comes to being on TV or radio, or how to give an inspirational quote so it makes the newspaper or magazine article.

And I haven't stopped producing shows. For one client, I produce her travel show. It airs on PBS worldwide. I dig up the stories, plan the shoots, find the interviews – direct the crew and show host – and then write the show for TV and the web. It's been fun flying to a few places I haven't seen. For the majority of my career, I spent an ungodly amount of hours each day inside a newsroom. It's nice to experience things in person – and not just through monitors in a control room.

That's what I help people do. I can't take credit for finding that myself. People started asking me for help – and I followed the demand. I listen to my customers and help them produce the results they want.

Congratulations on all your accomplishments and your Emmy Awards. That's very outstanding.

Could you share a little bit about the exact type of person that you help, entrepreneurs, business owners or people just starting out, could you go into that just a little bit deeper?

Kathryn Janicek: My typical client is a rock star at what they do. They're in their 30s, 40s, 50s and 60+. The two things they all have in common is they're an expert in their industry and they need to help translating their message to their audience to make sure their content sticks. I want audiences to feel energy and passion from my clients. Their target customer should be saying: "Wow! I want to work for that person," "I want to know that person," "I want to buy their book," or "I believe in that company."

I teach people how to present better so they can attract more clients. I produce the best YOU.

If they need more energy -- I help them inject that into their presentation skills. If they need help engaging their audience – I show them how to create more memorable messages. Sometimes they need more confidence so they can shine either at work or during a major presentation. I help with that too.

They learn how to breathe correctly, how to deliver their message, what to wear in different scenarios, ways their posture changes their message, how to alter their tone to change how the message is delivered, how and where to sit at a conference room table to demand authority, how to end and start sentences in an authoritative way, what colors to wear, how to carry

147

themselves on stage or during an interview, how to make a statement without going overboard when it comes to makeup (men too) and jewelry... and how to work with stage lighting. One of the biggest improvements I made with a client's overall presentation had to do with his eyebrows.

It's not just speeches. If a client is preparing for a job interview, we go through key points they need to land. Even if the hiring manager doesn't ask – we practice ways to make sure those messages are delivered and the employer sees the client's excellence.

I think people in their 30s, 40s, 50s and older get it. They say, "There's a reason I haven't been able to move up," "Maybe there's a reason I haven't been able to get my story out in the media or sell more," or "I'm a financial advisor like her - why haven't I been able to get into an article in Forbes or on a cable news segment?" And then they finally act on it and hire someone like me.

I would love to help more people who are just starting out, but usually it's by mentoring. Many people in their 20's, who really *need* the coaching respond, "You're x-amount per hour or x-amount per month? I really can't afford that." They haven't realized yet that you have to invest in yourself to come off as your best in an interview or during a presentation. I produce the best out of people and companies. That's a service worth paying for. People need to invest in themselves and this training earlier on so they can avoid performance mistakes - and develop fewer bad habits.

If we all could have been a better-produced version of ourselves in our 20s -- we might have worked up the career ladder a little faster.

There are so many pieces to landing a job. It's not just about being the smartest. You need to be the best-produced person. There's a lot of competition. There are many people with the same skills who are just as smart or smarter. It's the entire package that gets you the job. How you handle yourself in the interview – how you present when it comes to wardrobe and body language. We say so much with just how we LOOK.

That's why I created Intern with Intention.

Our mission is to help students turn their internships into JOBS. I love speaking at colleges. Small groups are the best. I help with their social media profiles, their digital branding, resumes... I also answer questions about what to wear at internships or interviews. I'm often shocked when I hear from seniors who are graduating that either haven't had an internship – or didn't know how seriously to take the internship. They never made the contacts there to help them land a job either at that company or somewhere else in the industry. I've seen interns get hired just because they were physically in the door and were doing a good job. Could the hiring manager have found someone more qualified for the job? Yes – but someone was there – and it was easier to fill the position with that person than to recruit and move someone to town. This happens all the time. I've given interns paid jobs after their internships. But, *they* did the work making themselves valuable. Writers are hired at TV stations from internships. They were just there when they were needed – and showed eagerness to learn and work hard.

Former interns reach out to me often asking how to handle a job negotiation, a contract and all the other things a 20-something-year-old person is never taught how to do. I'm honored that they come to me. Many students don't get enough advice from their teachers, parents, and counselors on how to land a job. I do a lot of college talks – but **Intern with Intention** will help mentor more students. I'm able to help MORE college students and young professionals. There's information on how to get involved at www.kathrynjanicek.com.

Awesome response. Thank you for that. You mentioned earlier that you'd been in this field twenty-some years. What got you

149

started twenty years ago and what led you to this field and how did you get started in this business?

Kathryn Janicek: I'm an anomaly because I knew what I wanted to do since junior high. I wrote for my school paper in seventh grade!

My parents were news lovers. We were a two-newspaper family.

We didn't watch a lot of TV – but we always watched the news. It was "Wheel of Fortune" and the news. That's what we were allowed to watch. My parents talked about politics and everything else in the news at the kitchen table – they still do. They're sponges. They love to learn and passed that onto us. It was great when I moved to Chicago in my 30's and produced at WGN and NBC. My audience was the Chicago metropolitan area, and that included my family. What an honor to present the news for your news-addicted family every morning! It was pretty exciting to read things at one in the morning before anyone else. I was the one who decided what my audience would learn when they woke up at five o'clock. I made sure they were prepared and knew what was going on in the world before they left for work or school.

I continued to write for school papers in high school, but when I started looking at colleges, I began to wonder how long the newspaper biz would be sustainable. This was twenty years ago... we had AOL email addresses. Things were a'changin'! People were creating websites for the first time.

I chose Marquette University in Milwaukee because it had an excellent broadcast journalism program. Plus – now, here's something imperative for high school students to think about... I wanted to go to a school where I could touch the equipment... take the classes in my major and kick the wheels my FRESHMAN year. I didn't want to wait until junior year to enter the journalism school like what was required at some of the other colleges I visited. What happens if you find out junior year - when you finally start taking classes in your major - that it's not your cup of tea?

I had a job offer a few weeks before I graduated from college. My parents loaded up a U-Haul and took me from school right to the first city I'd work in during my 20s. I was a morning show producer, and I dabbled in some reporting. It was *that* seamless going from college to my first job because I did the work during college. I already was producing news as a paid associate producer my junior and senior years at the FOX television station and the ABC radio station in Milwaukee. I had an internship right away freshman year - and I turned it into a job at another station. That's so important. You have to turn that internship into a job. It sounds silly – but you have to have experience to get that entry level job.

Once you have the job... it's all about learning as much as you can and moving on when it's time. After a year in Champaign, Illinois, I moved on. I never looked for a job; headhunters called me. "Can you come to Memphis to produce?" "Can you come to Detroit? Fox needs a producer." "Want to move to Minneapolis? KSTP needs an executive producer."

It was in my 30s when I first had to hunt for a job. I moved home to Chicago without a job lined up. I knew I wanted to work in TV in Chicago – it was home, and it was time. It could have been a terrible move, but the news directors at the FOX and NBC stations in town said, "The first executive producer opening we have is yours." I just had to hustle in the meantime.

At the time, LinkedIn was blowing up. Everyone was building their online network. It was perfect timing because I needed to build a Chicago network, and fast. It helped me find a few freelance jobs to work while I waited. I freelanced 6-7 days a week for the CBS news radio station in town – learning from the best in Chicago. I also produced newscasts for WGN-TV. When a job opened up at WGN, I took it. Then six months later one of the executive producer jobs I was waiting for opened up. I was the morning executive producer for NBC Chicago for about two and a half years.

My next TV gig was at a TV network that didn't even exist when I was hired. I was the fourth employee – and it was my first startup. It was the year when a ton of digital TV network startups popped up. It was an incredible experience. I got to hire dozens of people in a matter of months... producers, editors, writers and photographers. I'll never forget calling editors on Christmas Eve from O'Hare International Airport as I was flying out to see my parents in Florida – hiring people right over the phone. (I had already interviewed them in person.) I felt like Santa – or Oprah. You get a job! YOU get a job!

It was a very fast hiring process.

I loved teaching young professionals how to write news -- and editors who came from the documentary world how to cut a story in under an hour. There were extreme growing pains at first. I learned a lot about launching a company, and I was lucky to see how *not* to do things on many levels. They never promoted the content or sold it... or had a business plan. I'll never forget the arguments about the importance of social media ads. This is one of the reasons I ask clients now if they *want* to be the best. Going half of the way is not good enough. At the end of each day, I was proud of the amount of content my news team produced on an hourly/daily basis. They are too.

All this time – I had a burning desire to help more people by going out on my own. Like a lot of people, I had fear and lots of questions, like, "Will I be able to pay my rent?" Finally, I just went for it. I had all the support I needed. My family and friends weren't like, "what are you nuts?" They said, "Start your company. It's time." One even said I always reminded her of Bethenny Frankel (in the entrepreneurial take no prisoner's way... not the reality show "The Real Housewives of New York City" way). I'll take that.

You're lucky to have the support from your parents and friends. Others are not so lucky when they start the entrepreneurial journey.

Kathryn Janicek: A lot of people don't have that kind of support.

I surround myself with very smart people. I don't have the kind of friends who sit at bars and watch football on the weekends. We volunteer – we help lead charities – we sponsor tables – we mentor – we cheer each other on instead of trying to push each other down to look better. I love my friends – even when they have a crazy idea like doing a double-header spin class. They know what's best for me. They're incredible people.

It is definitely always better to uplift each other. Any other experience that shaped what you're doing now for your clients?

Kathryn Janicek: I was the spokesperson for a sheriff's department in the Minneapolis area for a year. I managed all the international, national and local press when the I-35W bridge collapsed over the Mississippi River. I was maybe three, four months on the job. I was getting used to being on call 24/7 – writing a lot of press releases and showing up whenever a body floated up in a lake. Then a bridge collapsed in the middle of the Mississippi River during rush hour – and killed 13 people. 145 people were hurt. It was the second busiest bridge in the entire state of Minnesota. Media from all over the world came – and it was just me and my blackberry managing all the calls. We weren't prepared for that level of crisis when it came to the communication.

Now – I teach people how to keep a clear head during a crisis.

Everyone from the local news to national – and then Al Jazeera and Polish newspapers were calling my blackberry within hours. Once I was allowed to start disseminating information – I ran news conferences hourly. Then the sheriff started giving my cell phone number LIVE over the air during press conferences... and he wanted to be on all the national news shows. It was a big job. I had friends bring me fresh clothing some days. Walmart's PR people brought food and deodorant. I can't remember sleeping. I worked from the crash site for a few days until we got a trailer with a fax machine and a desk. Next, the U.S. Navy Seals came with their crisis communications team. There were ego battles between the levels of law enforcement, but I loved how the communications people worked together so well.

This experience was crucial in my crisis communications training. I didn't just need to control the message - but I knew it was imperative that the media got what they needed. If they didn't – they went around us and got the wrong information. I had to fight to get the information out in a timely fashion. I made sure we were as honest as possible without damaging the investigation or releasing information before the victims' families received it. I was able to do that job better because I came from newsrooms.

That's what helps me coach people. I've been that spokesperson – the one writing the press release and delivering the news. I've also produced news, so I know what the media wants. I'm able to tell companies, "This is a good story in January," or, "This is an excellent story in June," or, "You could be on this network because they're doing this educational push right now." I know everything about the timing of a news story.

That's a lot of experience that you can bring to the table. Every entrepreneur that I interview always has been influenced by a person or a book. Is there any one person that's inspired you or a book along the way?

Kathryn Janicek: I don't even know where to start. I read a lot. I'm always devouring a few books... and listening to a few audiobooks. I'm listening to four right now including Gloria

Steinem's biography, "My Life on the Road." I heard her interview on NPR about it and downloaded it right away. My family had moved six times before I graduated high school (5 elementary schools)... and I thought I could relate a little to her transient childhood and adulthood. I've also read all of the comedian, Chelsea Handler's, books... so I don't know what that says about me. I gravitate toward biographies. I love to learn about people and hear their stories – in their voice. It's one of the reasons I got into journalism.

Okay, is there a person that you can think about that inspired you?

Kathryn Janicek: Inspired me ... There's so many.
The most important are my parents.

I grew up in a household with parents who had a very critical eye for how things SHOULD be. A grocery shopping experience with my mom was never without a lesson in customer service. You'd be in line, and she was watching the bagger with one eye. With the other, she watched each item as it came up on the screen. She knew all the prices and double checked the computer. With another eye (don't moms have like 5?) she peered at the conveyor belt. Was it wet? She also knew if the person checking the groceries greeted her – or said "thank you" at the end of the transaction. Oh, and she also kept an eye on her three daughters. Her background in training employees on how to be the best rubbed off on me.

My father is the same – but at bars and restaurants. He spent decades improving brands, businesses and salespeople. It's frustrating to him when he can see obvious elements that could be tweaked to give the customer a better experience. The food doesn't need to be over the top... but if the server seems like she cares, if he has good timing... if she's just more aware of what's going on around her... that can make a huge difference in the customer's experience. It needs to be an experience… not just good food. We can eat at home – but we choose to go out to enjoy a moment and possibly learn something new. If you're going to open up for business – be a pro. Be ready for your customers.

My parents' awareness of their surroundings and how businesses could perform better shaped me. People who have worked for me have said that it's sometimes difficult because my eye is on everything. I never wanted an imperfect story to hit the ears or eyes of a viewer. I wanted a real experience. I watched if the necklace was out of place for my anchor, if there was a hair out of place, if he looked tired – if that white dress not right.

If a woman, for example, is on stage and she has lots of bracelets and a necklace -- my eye is on that because if any of it starts hitting her microphone – she's toast. People don't realize how much that detracts from their message and the experience they give their audience. I think I've been finely aware of that since I was maybe five, four years old because my parents were so aware. I just soaked it up unconsciously.

It's made me superb at my job because I can gravitate towards something immediately that might be an issue for someone's audience or their customers. I try to either work with it or make it go away. At first, the client is surprised – because no one's told them their eyebrows or the frames of their glasses crowd their eyes and make them look untrustworthy… but once they fix it – they SEE it. I love seeing the reaction and the happiness. They're more CONFIDENT – and they show it on stage and in front of their teams. It's a big win for both of us.

I was coaching someone recently, and her hair was in front of her face. It kept dropping in front of her eye. I had to explain to her that it would detract from her message. She was a little put-off … but I talked her through how the audience would be focused on her hair instead of how brilliant she was. It's not the audience's intention. It's just how we naturally think. It's unfortunate, but if there's an issue with her physical

156

presentation -- it will become more important than her actual content.

Recently, a client asked me how I learned it. "How do you notice all this stuff?" I have to credit my parents. They made me more aware – and it makes my clients better because of it. If the audience is distracted -- their message isn't received. It's that simple.

It's all in the details, right?

Kathryn Janicek: It's all in the details. There's information that claims 80% of your content comes from your body language and the colors you're wearing and whatever else can distract your audience. If we can eliminate all those distractions, the audience will hear and absorb your content.

It's paramount that a restaurant has the best ambiance that befits their food. The food isn't going to taste great if the waiter isn't on his game that night and makes you feel welcome.

If a speaker's necklace is hitting her microphone or her lipstick is a little distracting, or his tie is crooked, or his pants are baggy at the bottom - we're drawn to that. And it makes that expert look sloppy and less credible. That can blow it for somebody. That's why I love coaching those mid- to high-level executives because sometimes these small tweaks can help them move up more quickly. It helps their credibility instantly. Sometimes I can fix it in a day, sometimes it's a couple of weeks or months, but it helps their credibility big time.

A lot of people that haven't been in the military, for instance, they might not experience that detail aspect of it.

Kathryn Janicek: Yeah. We learn a lot in school – but beyond what we know – is the message we're giving the public about *what* we know. We may not be sloppy at our job – but if we LOOK sloppy, does that recruiter think we won't pay attention to the details of the work?

I wish schools trained us better on manners, delivery, interviewing... there are refinements we could use to help us with our careers. I have volunteered for years for a charity that helps military veterans and their families go to college. I've watched how these veterans carry themselves. It's beautiful. That's training everyone should have.

Exactly. Talk about what drives you. What gives you your passion and to do what you do to help people that you help?

Kathryn Janicek: The fact that I like helping people. I get calls from colleges (and this doesn't help my checking account at all... but it helps my "Feel Good" checking account) all the time. Last month, I was at a major university -- and I sat for an hour and helped seven or eight college women with their LinkedIn pages. We perfected their headlines and I talked to them about how important it is to turn their internships into jobs... what to wear and what not to wear in their profile pictures online and how to clean up their social media.

I like seeing the change. It's kind of like when I edit a piece for TV, a blog post or their web content - I like seeing that positive change. I like knowing I helped someone. It makes me feel good. I get an enormous high out of it. I coached a brilliant woman recently. She has a master's and a Ph.D. -- but there were things that I knew that she didn't, and it helped her boost her confidence, and it's going to help her present better in the media and front of major conference rooms. I love that I was able to help her.

I will say I've had young producers who didn't love working with me at the time. I want the best out of each person, but they don't realize when they're in it - that I'm trying to make them better. They thank me later. I received a note from someone a few years ago that I will never forget. When she worked for me – it was her first English-speaking television station. She came from Telemundo and was used to writing scripts in Spanish. I wasn't "tough" on her – I just held her to the same standards as the other producers. I don't believe in "sink or swim" because I didn't want her to sink... I wanted her to swim and swim really strong. I knew she had a goal – and that was to be on-air. I needed her to be the best writer she could be. There was no other option. Months after she landed her first on-air reporting job – at an English-speaking station -- she sent me a thank you message. It's knowing that I made a difference that motivates me. I want to make people better. I CARE.

Yeah, there you go. That moves into our next question. What is the biggest misconception that you're finding with your clients?

Kathryn Janicek: That I'm just going to tell them how to breathe from their diaphragm and maybe rewrite a little bit of their presentation. One client thought I was just going to come in and help them read their presentation better, go through their PowerPoint and help them fix it up. When I started asking the exec, "Why are you doing that with your hands? What colors are you going to wear? What shoes? Jeans or slacks? What's the audience wearing? What did prior presenters wear?" He replied, "Oh, my God. I didn't even think about that. I don't know."

I think they're surprised with the attention to detail. I ask, "Where's the microphone going to be? Where are the cameras? Is it going to be a lavaliere mic or is it going to be a stick mic? Will this be on the web later?" When they respond, "I didn't think about that" – I fill in the blanks for them. I find out the answers so I can prepare them. That's my job.

I think about the entire experience for the audience and how they're going to look at the audience that's live there in the seats and to the greater audience on the web later.

Can you describe one of your clients, without naming them, but how you've helped them, take them from A to B to overcome those obstacles? Can you give us a short story?

Kathryn Janicek: One of my first clients didn't even hire me. His team did. They knew he was a rock star at what he does – but his presentation skills were lacking. He didn't show passion in his presenting. I don't know if he wanted my help at first, but in the end – it was a great experience. I brought more life to his delivery and the actual presentation. I received feedback after the event that he felt more confident. Practice – which brings confidence - is sometimes all we need to perform better.

When I coached a team of execs from one company – I noticed the confidence the men had when presenting. When a female manager who was their equal got up to rehearse, she didn't bring the same bravado. She seemed weak and her confidence issues made her come off as if she didn't know what she was talking about. For her, it was all about giving her the confidence. When it comes to presenting – you have to walk up knowing that you own it and that you're an expert at what you do. Sometimes I just need to pump people up because they're really good, and they know their material inside out, but they're scared to show it.

Women have been historically taught not to brag. Men can boast. Women feel as if they just need to get the job done and not make waves. That's crazy. It's okay to bring attention toward yourself – especially when you HAVE to on stage.

I've also coached people who never knew the way they breathe made them come off as being nervous in front of their smaller teams – and in front of bigger audiences.

Then there are the fast talkers. They know the content in and out – and they're passionate, loud and super energetic on stage. The problem? No one can understand them because they talk so fast! You can't absorb all the information spewing from their brains. I help bring them down a little when it comes to the rate of speed – without losing all that wonderful passion!

What would be the best piece of advice that you'd give someone who's considering a speaking career or using the media to advance their career?

Kathryn Janicek: Have a relatable story. You have to have a story people can relate to if you're going to get up and present or if you're going to try to sell your business in the media. It needs to be a story that sells. It needs to be compelling.

Remember: the media has a job to do – and that's to make sure their audience watches, reads, sticks with them, learns something and keeps coming back for more. Give the media something good to work with – and you'll have a chance.

Also, find out who's looking for that story, so you're not just sending out press releases to everyone. There will be media outlets that don't even do your kind of story or that don't book people like you as guests or experts. You need to know your media audience – just like you know your audience of customers.

At the end of the day - the most important thing is to have a relatable story whether you're giving a presentation about your company, trying to get yourself into the news, or hoping to get booked on stage as an expert. There has to be a relevant story.

Great advice! How can readers contact you and learn more about what you do?

Kathryn Janicek: You can find me on Twitter, Instagram or LinkedIn with the handle: @KathrynJanicek. I'm on Facebook here: https://www.facebook.com/kathrynjanicek1 and you can email me at kathryn@kathrynjanicek.com.

For an overview of my services, please go to my website at http://www.kathrynjanicek.com. If you upload a video – I'll give you on-the-spot coaching!

WEBSITE:
http://www.kathrynjanicek.com

EMAIL:
kathryn@kathrynjanicek.com.

FACEBOOK:
www.facebook.com/kathrynjanicek1

LINKEDIN:
www.linkedin.com/in/kathrynjanicek

YOUTUBE:
http://www.youtube.com/c/KathrynJanicek

PHONE:
(312) 545-6480

CLOSING THOUGHTS

Now that you've made it all the way to the end, I applaud you.

Most people, who purchase books, never make it past the first chapter. You now have the proverbial, "keys to the kingdom" of how to make this year your best year ever.

All success in life starts with you. You know what to do. You know how to do it. Your next step is simple. Start taking massive action toward your goals and dreams.

On behalf of the rest of the authors who've collaborated on Success Hackers, we wish you success, prosperity, abundance, growth, and significance in your life and business.

Be Great Today!

Scott Hansen

75310269R00095

Made in the USA
San Bernardino, CA
27 April 2018